The Cup of Blessing

The Cup of Blessing

Looking at the Background to Holy Communion in St. John's Gospel

TODDY HOARE

Foreword by Peter Sedgwick

WIPF & STOCK · Eugene, Oregon

THE CUP OF BLESSING
Looking at the Background to Holy Communion in St. John's Gospel

Wipf & Stock
An Imprint of Wipf and Stock Publishers
199 W. 8th Ave., Suite 3
Eugene, OR 97401

www.wipfandstock.com

PAPERBACK ISBN: 979-8-3852-7634-9
HARDCOVER ISBN: 979-8-3852-7635-6
EBOOK ISBN: 979-8-3852-7636-3

VERSION NUMBER 03/03/26

Front cover: Photo of chalice. This is the chalice made from a shattered whisky tumbler that inspired the theme of this book. Cast in bronze by TH and gilded with gold inside to make it safe to drink from.

Back cover: The same image of my chalice to reach a wider audience using a printed linocut by TH to catch attention and speak differently from a photo by encouraging a different response.

To Arthur Moore, who taught me New Testament studies at Wycliffe Hall, and Leslie Stanbridge, who presented me for ordination at York Minster to a ripple of laughter all round, and who encouraged his clergy to continue studies and attempt writing a commentary.

The Cup of Blessing

God's cup of wrath had an accumulation
A reflection of His pent-up frustration
With creation deserving its presentation
To drain it without interception
As their judgment and damnation.
What Son of Adam or Daughter of Eve
Could by drinking salvation achieve
Causing the cup's curse's cancellation?
The Son of Man accepted the dedication
Giving thanks with the cup's consecration
To offer all accepting eternal preservation.
Yet in Gethsemane a moment of hesitation:
'Let this cup pass, nay thy will be done.'
Thus light shone, the Kingdom was won.

Revd. Toddy Hoare.
Danby Wiske, North Yorkshire.
St. Bride's Day, 10th February 2026.

Contents

Foreword

One of the greatest works of theology in English in the twentieth century was Austin Farrer's *The Glass of Vision*, published in 1948, which was a book that provoked a great deal of criticism.[1] Farrer argued that God's revelation is not through propositions, even one such as "God is love," nor through events, but rather through images, and as events are recalled, remembered and re-presented they become an image in their own right. This does not deny that events are not of supreme importance, such as the incarnation, crucifixion and resurrection of the one whom Jeremy Taylor, a seventeenth century Anglican bishop, theologian and poet called "the holy Jesus,"[2] but rather that our knowledge of events is through the images they present to us in our minds now. Such events and images are found above all for a Christian in the words of Holy Scripture, and again the response to scripture should be as much literary as analytic. Farrer also stressed the importance of poetry and one of his chapters (originally a lecture) is entitled "Poetry and the New Testament." In all of this the role of imagination is crucial, and it is provocative but profoundly true to say that the Christian as he/she encounters God has in their scriptural reading and prayers to "imagine the truth." Imagination is the great gift

1. Austin Farrer, *The Glass of Vision* (London: A and C Black, 1948).

2. Jeremy Taylor, "The History of the Life and Death of the Holy Jesus." In *The Whole Works of the Right Rev. Jeremy Taylor*, edited by Reginald Heber, revised by Charles Page Eden (repr., Hildesheim: George Olms, 1970).

which God has given us, and the work of the Holy Spirit uses our imagination that He "will guide you into all truth" (John 16:3).

Imagination is Toddy's great gift, the imagination of a down-to-earth ex-soldier, a country parson for decades, a passionate sculptor, and in recent years a prolific writer and poet. As a friend for well over thirty years, I see him in his Leake vicarage with a painting over the fireplace in dark and somber colors of armored cars in Belfast during the Troubles, recalling his service there;[3] I see him with farmers out on the moors in his old Range Rover car, ready to lend a hand mending a tractor; I see him in a medieval country church, taking Evensong. His life has been a wonderful combination of intense practicality and imagination, knowing intensely the lie of the land, the animals and the fields, in the countryside of the North Yorkshire Moors which was for so long his parish, or understanding how to work in metal, and yet having the visionary eye of the artist. As U.A. Fanthorpe wrote in her celebrated poem *Atlas:*

> There is a kind of love called maintenance
> Which stores the WD40 and knows when to use it [. . .]
> And maintenance is the sensible side of love,
> Which knows what time and weather are doing
> To my brickwork'[4]

Toddy has cared for innumerable individuals whose "brickwork" has been severely damaged by illness, the storms of life, and much else, and brought God's love alongside them. He writes, "In acting for him, the Spirit moves us, because in order to be of comfort to anyone we must draw alongside that person first, whether a bereaved neighbor, a starving child, those in hospital or prison, the AIDS victim and the stranger."

In a publication twenty years ago, co-authored with his wife Liz, on *Sculpture, Prayer and Scripture*, Toddy wrote, "Artists have a particular way of seeing the world, and they invite us to see it

3. See the allusions to his military service in chapters 13 and 15, and military service in general and the losses of war in chapter 10.

4. U. A. Fanthorpe, "Atlas." In U. A. Fanthorpe, *Safe as Houses* (N. p.: Peterloo Poets, 1995).

in a new way for ourselves. . . to become better in touch with reality, and also with God, who is in all things, beautiful or otherwise. . . He (Toddy) would claim to be a Prayer Book Anglican, someone for whom the words of the *Book of Common Prayer* and the Bible have been in his bloodstream since childhood. His meditations on Scripture find physical expressions through his hands, working first in clay and subsequently in bronze."[5] This was written in 2004, and since then he has used his imagination in writing poetry, as well as sculpture. However, the two forms of expression in sculpture and poetry are closely linked. "Sculpture, like poetry, is an art form which relies on allusion, metaphor, imagery and occasionally paradox." Sculpture, like Jesus preaching the Kingdom of God, depends on allusion, and "an invitation to imagine how things are, and, if we will, to move on how things might be."[6]

The meditations in this book on St. John's Gospel are in prose, though very different from *Uncle Peter's Story*,[7] and quite unlike his earlier *Psalmody*[8] and *The Christ Cycle*.[9] However the symbolism is just as intense, as it is in his earlier poetry, and imagery, symbolism, event and response pervade the whole work, echoing this Gospel, which is the most reflective of all the Gospels. It is extraordinary that this study was first conceived by a rural parish priest with all the pressures on his life, yet this is how it came to be, because it was initially created as part of Toddy's in-service clergy training, and the sheer intensity of these chapters shows a mind steeped in the verses of John's Gospel. It may well be, as in his earlier publication on sculpture and prayer, that you need to take time over each chapter and allow the dense alliteration to permeate your heart and mind, and move you to adoration and gratitude for

5. Liz Culling and Toddy Hoare, *Sculpture, Prayer and Scripture* (Cambridge: Grove Spirituality Series, 2004), 3–4.

6. Culling and Hoare, *Sculpture, Prayer and Scripture*, 8.

7. Toddy Hoare, *Uncle Peter's Story* (Eugene, OR: Resource, 2025).

8. Toddy Hoare, *Psalmody* (Eugene, OR: Resource, 2024).

9. Toddy Hoare, *The Christ Cycle in Verse and 3D* (Eugene, OR: Resource, 2025).

what is shown here, where the cup of wrath (Isa 51:17) becomes the cup of blessing (1 Cor 10:16).

For Toddy, Jesus is "the wineglass at the wedding ceremony, broken on the cross so to speak," where the symbolism of the broken glass at a Jewish wedding is taken up in the chalice Toddy made out of a broken glass, which is pictured on the cover of this book.

For my fortieth birthday I was given rather a fine antique glass whisky tumbler which some years later met with an accident. Reflecting on the pieces beyond repair, I cast it in bronze as a chalice because it told a story. Having gilded the inside in gold, it does get used. (See same on cover picture.) As a sculptor and a parish priest it was a useful illustration as it represented the Old Testament cup of judgment becoming the New Testament cup of salvation.

Chalice and cup are intertwined in this book. There are no less than forty-seven meditations on the word "cup" and seven on "chalice." The Latin for cup is *calix*, and this became in Old French *chalice*. By 1382 Wycliffe was translating Genesis 40:13 as "*Thow shalt ȝyue to hym* a *chalice, after thin office*," and by 1882 the Victorian poet William Bell Scott could write, "*Life is God's chalice filled with tears*."[10] But life is not like that for Toddy in this book. While there is no avoiding the harshness and sorrow of life, this is a book about the profundity of salvation, a meditation on the Eucharistic chalice (or cup) of blessing, the new life which Jesus brings. Read it—slowly—and let your imagination be moved in the depths of your being by this reflection on the action of the Son of God as revealed to us in the images and symbols of St. John's Gospel. It is a book to be read and re-read as an introduction to the Gospel, a springboard to further study, a meditative reflection on the symbolism of the Christian faith.

Peter Sedgwick
St Nicholas, Vale of Glamorgan, Wales.
November 14, 2025

10. William Bell Scott, *A Poet's Harvest Home*, (N.p.: Forgotten Books, 2018).

Preface

WHEN WE CAN RELATE spiritual things to our own experience, we are enriched. I believe there is an aspect of St John's Gospel we overlook but which is there to help us relate this remarkable gospel more intimately to ourselves. I have puzzled often over the Wedding at Cana at the start of chapter 2, yet here is a key to approaching and entering the gospel and our Christian life in a particular way. Indeed the request made at the wedding reflects the nature of our own frequent prayer requirements. Historically we can only speculate at whose nuptials took place: Nathanael of Cana, found by his friend and told of Jesus in the previous chapter? Indeed, what was he doing under the fig tree? Had he just proposed?! Was it our Lord himself getting married? Unlikely, as his mother calls upon him to help, so that his moment is suddenly sprung upon him from others. The bridegroom to whom the steward bears the new wine from after being changed is a different person. As a fact it does not matter because spiritually the groom is Christ, the Lamb of God, as indicated by John the Baptist—the best man, if you like—and the bride is us, the Church. We are drawn, therefore, into a very intimate relationship. The symbolism of John's Gospel can be applied yet further if we consider the ritual surrounding a Jewish wedding and take our cue from an event that John places so strategically at the start of his narrative.

At a Jewish wedding the focus of the action is round the glass of wine, blessed and presented to the bride and groom, who then drink it. On completion the groom breaks the glass. Again, through this gospel narrative Jesus becomes the glass and the wine; in fact is present in all the activity of the wedding. It is his body which is broken and emptied just as when the wine glass is destroyed.

THE JEWISH WEDDING CEREMONY

The wedding takes place under a chuppah—a canopy. There are readings from the scriptures; a first cup of wine with blessings; the ring and exchanges of vows; the reading and signing of the marriage contract or the ketubah; Seven Blessings and the second cup of wine, which again both bride and groom drink; then finally the groom crushes the wineglass with his heel.

Here we enter into a lot of symbolism. If we think of the canopy as the tent covering the Law of Moses in the Old Testament, there is the sense of the bride, us the Church, being joined to the groom, Christ, in a new relationship. A wedding ring symbolizes the everlasting link from the beginning to the end. As to the contract, we find that in Jesus' teaching through the gospel and in baptism. In the destruction of the glass there is a symbol for destroying all that is bad and enjoying a fresh start. When we think of the body of Christ actually being the wine glass, the vessel from which the blood is poured, again we see our own fresh start through his resurrection and a new relationship with God.

Taking the chapters of St John's Gospel as found in the R.S.V, I would extract the following pattern:

JOHN'S GOSPEL CHAPTER BY CHAPTER

1. Introduction. The Word made flesh. Of Genesis.
   John's Witness.
   Four disciples find and accept Jesus.

2. The *Marriage* of Cana.
   The temple cleansed. A new relationship before God started.

3. New *birth.*
   Nicodemus
   Baptism.
   John's witness: (a sort of best man!)
   3:29–30. "He who has the bride is the bridegroom: the friend of the bridegroom, who stands and hears him, rejoices greatly at the bridegroom's voice: therefore this joy of mine is now full."

4. Samaria. Living water. Water mixed in the cup.
   4:24. God is Spirit, and those who worship him must worship in spirit and truth.

5. Healing—and more commentary on John 5:33–.

6. Feeding five thousand and the *Bread* of Life.
   Jesus walks on the water: essence of Baptism when we take Jesus on board.
   Confrontation.

7. Feast of Tabernacles: Living Water

8. *Adultery.* Him without sin may cast first stone.
   A new relationship.
   Lux Mundi, Light of the World: Manifestation of Jesus leads to understanding the Groom. We are The Children of Abraham.

9. Blind man healed.

10. *Jesus the Good Shepherd* (his employment). I am the way in (Gate).
    10:22–24: Jesus the Christ the Son of God.

11. Raising of Lazarus. (New life ahead in Jesus). *Resurrection and life.*

12. Jesus anointed.
    Palm Sunday: Walk while you have the light: Eternal life.
    Many passages continue to describe the Groom.

13. Service and example.
    Washing disciples' feet.

14. *Way, truth and life.*
    The Holy Spirit: living in the power and strength of the Father: the blessing.
15. *The true* vine. (*Blood/wine that fills the cup*).
16. Holy Spirit/Comforter.
17. The three-part prayer.
    1. Self
    2. Friends
    3. The bride
18. *The cup is broken.*
    Betrayal and arrest. Interrogation before Pilate.
19. Crucifixion, and death and burial.
    19:34: pierced with spear, at once there came out blood and water.
20. Resurrection. Do not cling to me (hold me back). My Lord and my God.
    19:28–29: Blessed are those who have not seen and believe.
21. Big catch: Peter and John

Introduction

THIS COMMENTARY IS THE accumulation of years of study for parish sermons and for the background to scriptures I have tackled as subject matter for sculptures. My object all sublime when preaching is to make people think, and I have set out to take that further by hanging St. John's Gospel on the idea of a marriage, and expanding on the description of us, the Church, as the bride of Christ, the bridegroom. It is akin to well-matured whisky that has sat in a barrel, for this manuscript has mellowed for a number of years on my desk. Noticing how there is a thirst for more teaching at a congregational level when I preach, I dare release the fruits of my ponderings on the wider church. Thus I am grateful to years of commentary from C.H. Dodd, R.H. Lightfoot, William Temple and W. Barclay, all before my time; Stuart Blanch, George Caird, Anthony Hanson and Anthony Harvey, all of whom taught me; and latterly those contributions from R.E.O. White and Tom Wright. There are countless other snippets, commentaries, bits from lectures and talks from the likes of Rowan Williams which suggest one can never get enough and that one should read everything that comes within reach or hearing, including a good sermon, and Credo in *The Times* on Saturdays!

Thus this commentary is a distillation of my thoughts on John, the spiritual gospel, on which I have drawn when called upon to preach.

It could be seen as a gentle gallop through the gospel on a particular steed!

Blessed are you Lord God of all creation. Through your goodness we have this wine to offer, fruit of the vine and the work of human hands. May it become for us the cup of salvation. Blessed be God for ever.

Chapter 1

THE INTRODUCTION

It is those familiar words used at Christmas that introduce us to the groom and his pedigree. The Word, made flesh, came to dwell (or literally tabernacle) amongst us. Not the long genealogies of Matthew and Luke, but here is the Word of God in human form. Given Jesus as the Word, there is a sense of God directly calling us as His creation continues in the idiom of His speaking in Genesis. God said, “Let there be light” (Gen 3). In verse 14 the Word became flesh and dwelt (tented) amongst us. Once more we enter the canopy, and is not a wedding a glorious day for both parties? An excuse for a party and celebration too!

John 1:12 = Rom 8:16. We are the children of God. Sonship comes through Christ.

Rather as a best man reciting the groom’s credentials, we have John bearing witness to Jesus, not only as light (v.8), but as the person of the Messiah anticipated by Isaiah (chapter 40), and as the Lamb of God (v.29). If we relate the Lamb of God to Isa 53:7, a sacrificial lamb, indeed a failure, then there is another side to be seen if translated thus: “He was praying, and he was answered, and before he opened his mouth he was accepted.”[1] Here, too, we are told by John that the Spirit descended as a dove from heaven. Representing the Old Testament, John points to the light.

1. A. T. Hanson, *The Prophetic Gospel* (Continuum International, 2000).

Pointed in the right direction of Jesus, Andrew sets off after Him and answers Him, calling, "Rabbi." Both Andrew and Philip say they have found the Messiah, and we meet both in the context and challenge of feeding the five thousand (6:5, 8).

John, as best man, gives his testimony to Jesus and points others in His direction. They in turn find others. Andrew goes to find his brother Peter (Cephas, the Rock).

Philip finds Nathanael/Bartholomew. They all accept Jesus and recognize Him for who He is. Thus the groom is presented and supported. In a way this spans the gap between priest and people, for on the former falls the responsibility of pointing the latter in Jesus' direction, of finding the latter and seeking them out. So while we are all Christ's bride within the church, others have a special task in the initial stages, but do not let this compromise the concept of the priesthood of all believers (1 Pet 2:9) and our work together to explain and celebrate the good news. Example, encouragement (after the manner of Barnabas: Acts 4:36) and exclamation of Jesus falls to us all. No mention of fishermen here, but they could have been working the Jordan near where John baptized, hence Andrew was able to find Peter.

The incident with Nathanael under the fig tree is very thought provoking. The fig tree was the symbol of Israel.

What was Nathanael doing? Picking figs? Saying his prayers? Chatting up his girlfriend or whatever prior to the wedding at Cana? Or making his confession? In verse 47 the description of him as being "an Israelite indeed, in whom there is no *guile*" leads me to Ps 32:6: "Blessed is the man to whom the Lord imputes no iniquity and in whose spirit there is no guile" (deceit). It is a penitent's psalm v.5: "I acknowledged my sin to thee, and I did not hide my iniquity; I said, 'I will confess my transgressions to the Lord,' and thou didst forgive the guilt of my sin." Verses 3 and 4 suggest this confession is not without effort and we can picture Nathanael spreadeagled under the tree. Perhaps he was watering his trees (v.6), or there had been a flood! Whatever, he found deliverance, otherwise he would not have so readily accepted Jesus as knowing something of his inner thoughts. In verses 8 and 9, instruction and teaching follow. Perhaps Nathanael's loaded mule was being obstinate (v.9). The picture we can conjure up is not lacking humor. Forgiveness was assured: "Blessed is he whose transgression is forgiven, whose sin is covered."

Somewhere in this picture of Nathanael under the fig tree there is a suggestion of a ladder. It could certainly have been in use if he was picking figs, a single central pole with rungs lashed or nailed to it. Such a visual image is prompted by Jesus' remark that closes the chapter: "You will see heaven opened and the angels ascending and descending upon the Son of Man." This suggests Jacob's dream at Bethel (Gen 28:10–end). So Nathanael is promised greater things, the relationship of the new Israel in all her number. Here was a promise indeed that was to be fulfilled. You can also read into it that Jesus is telling Nathanael that the prophecy in Mic 4:2–4 is fulfilled. NB: Jacob was full of guile until he was renamed Israel at Jabbok, where he found himself and his relationship to God and his brother Esau in a ritual akin to the mechanics of baptism (Gen 29).

Chapter 2

VERSES 1–12

HERE WE COME TO the main theme I would like to explore spiritually. John mentions a wedding, and as soon as we enter into the event we can view John's gospel in a new dimension. None of the synoptics mention this occasion, yet here Jesus is called by His mother when people are in need. He responds and so manifests His glory. Looking at the wedding from the spiritual point of view of Jesus being our groom, there is a certain irony over His changing water into wine whereby our chalice is filled. In the light of Jesus being the wineglass at the wedding ceremony, broken on the cross so to speak in chapter 19, and the water and the wine, it picks up with the imagery of His side being pierced at death so "at once there came out blood and water" (19:34). Again this is the living water, whereby Jesus also refers to himself. That is also a link to Jesus' pierced side with Adam's rib that was removed to become Eve.

VERSES 13–END

From a wedding, to the temple to cleanse it. This deed is put at the end of Jesus' ministry in the other gospels, after the triumphal entry into Jerusalem with all the pilgrims (Matt 21:12–17; Mark 11:15–19; Luke 19:45–48). However again this can fit our theme of celebrating a wedding and embarking on a new relationship. Marriage is about new relationships, so it seems appropriate that

Jesus goes to the heart of the matter when a new contract is made and clears the way. A good reason for His zeal is in verse 17. Trade had replaced prayer in the temple (the synoptics go as far as saying so explicitly). A real relationship with God is dependent on prayer, and it is prayer that uplifts a wedding and its participants to God.

Ironically, in verse 19 ("Destroy the temple and in three days I will raise it up") Jesus answers the Jews with the very words they were to hold against Him (Matt 26:60; 27:40 also predicted in psalms as false witnesses 27:12, 35:4). But John reminds us that these words later made sense to the disciples after the resurrection.

Despite His first sign, Jesus was not ready as He would not trust himself to men (again a theme found in John, when some would make Him king after feeding the five thousand (6:15)). Here is the groom wrestling with the human nature of others. He was here to witness to God and through that assurance give more hope.

Chapter 3

Nicodemus comes by night to question Jesus. In fact he became quite a fan—see John 7:50 when he spoke up in favor of Jesus: "Does our law judge a man without first giving him a hearing and learning what he does?" His colleagues sent him packing: "Are you from Galilee too?" Like Nathanael they could see no good in this hillbilly (Amos got a similar reception in the Old Testament). In 19:39 Nicodemus, along with Joseph of Arimathea, came with one hundred pounds of myrrh and aloes to bury Jesus' body.

Following the marriage, so to speak, at the start of our theme John takes the opportunity to open out a dialogue on birth, the fruit of any marriage. Again, the church to continue has to bring others to faith and help them understand this spiritual birth. Interestingly enough the mechanics of spiritual birth are the same as those of natural birth so that it falls within our experience and comprehension. When any mammal is born, except a duck-billed platypus, the waters break and on leaving its mother the newborn's first requirement is air. So too after baptism the requirement is to receive Holy Spirit as Jesus did at the start of this gospel. At its end He says, "Receive Holy Spirit" (20:22) and breathes on His disciples.

It is worth reflecting on the symbolism of the elements of baptism. Water sustains life not only in the womb, but generally. Indeed we are eighty percent water, but whether they knew any more than displacement of our own volume of water (Archimedes) is debatable. Arbitrary rain east of Jerusalem in the wilderness causes life suddenly to sprout. Hence the flocks are led from pasture to pasture. Water washes and cleanses, the other side of irrigation. Also, water quenches fire or drowns life. Here consider the ancient Jews undergoing a baptism as they left Egypt and passing through the Red Sea. Again, the same nation a generation later pass through the Jordan, another baptism prior to entering the promised land. Those favored by God passed through. Those displeasing to God, the Egyptians, were overwhelmed and blotted out the first time at the Red Sea. It is a sobering (!) thought that oblivion or nothing is the alternative to baptism and choosing God. Should we not try to encourage others a little harder? God is Spirit, so what there is of Him in us returns on our demise as mortals when we shed our physical shell.

By stretching the point that air = wind then again the idiom is helped because "wind" in Hebrew and Greek also can be translated "spirit." Here are the ingredients of baptism. Not all plain sailing and comfort, for the Spirit is there to stir up or disturb. Recall the sailor's adage, "Wind against tide, you're in for a rough ride." Friction results. So, too, baptism in its basic early form demands a response. The Holy Spirit demands action. Descriptions as Comforter or Counselor suggest that the appeal of the Holy Spirit responds by actions—drawing alongside the needy to comfort or counsel.

I find it highly significant that Jesus then proceeds to baptize people. Again it is worth reviewing John at work, for again at the end of this chapter John bears witness to Jesus once more and points us in the direction of being the true fruit of Christ's union with His church.

There is a sense that because John baptized down in the Jordan near Jericho, on being baptized and leaving the water the individual entered the promised land himself. Furthermore, if we take note of the synoptic gospels, John's cry was to "Repent and be baptized" (Matt 3:11; Luke 3:3); the literal image of "repent" is to turn round. Again, to enter and to leave the water after baptism the individual had to turn round. Life is more challenging to take a new direction, and Christianity again and again leaves us vulnerable but calls us on. We are not left just standing at a crossroads.

But having repented and turned round we recross our old ways, and in doing so have to recognize and review past life and come to terms with it. Not easy. Often it may mean making our peace! It is the bottom line of love and forgiveness. (Again, think of Jacob at Jabbok faced with encountering Esau.)

Mark is very telling when he writes (1:15) that Jesus preached the gospel of God and said, "The time is fulfilled, and the kingdom of God is at hand; repent and believe in the gospel" (good news). He moves on from John's sense of re-entering the promised land to entering the kingdom of God. That kingdom is not bounded by borders, patrolmen with dogs, wire, check points and customs men etc. It knows no barriers except the failure of our full response, for the kingdom of God is wherever "Thy kingdom come, thy will be done." Where we are obedient and pleasing to God (Luke 2:14: angel chorus to the shepherds) then we are in His kingdom. Matthew has John ushering in the kingdom of heaven on repenting (Matt 3:2), so it is worth comparing how the synoptic gospels treat John, his baptism and teaching, and Jesus' baptism, temptation and use of baptism himself. John makes the aside that Jesus did not baptize himself (4:2), when commenting on Jesus increasing and John the Baptist decreasing (3:25–36).

Another part of John's testimony to Jesus can be seen as life with the groom. 3:36 would be John the writer's own comment in conclusion: "He who believes in the Son has eternal life."

VERSES 16–21

John's own commentary on Jesus features here: an extra testimony rather than perhaps a continuation of Jesus' dialogue with Nicodemus as some suggest. We must be constrained to take the text as we find it in the absence of other texts. The light reveals people's deeds and what is good is wrought of God. Reflecting on Holman Hunt's picture of Lux Mundi, it is difficult not to lump together in the mind many of John's comments alongside what he gives us in Rev 3:20: "Behold I stand at the door and knock"—that anyone who responds in the Spirit will be joined by Jesus. Again, a further contrast of the groom with the ordinary run of men and their doings. John's first epistle begins with a commentary on the nature of responding to the light.

The words of 3:16 will also be familiar to many from the Holy Communion service where they constitute part of the "Comfortable Words." Here is the promise of eternal life through belief in the only Son, who was sent to save the world. The commentary raises our hope that we are not condemned because of our belief. Rather judgment, on which there is further comment by Jesus in 5:27, happens now depending on the individual's response to Jesus: either He is accepted as Son of God, light of the world, or He is rejected and the individual remains in the dark. What is done in the Son's name is recognizable as being wrought in God and the barriers of darkness are pushed back. In 3:3, Nicodemus came by night but saw the light. In 13:30, when Judas is given the morsel at the Last Supper and goes out with Jesus' knowledge, it was night. Judas went into the dark away from light.

Chapter 4

WE COME NOW TO the very example of a complete outsider who is won over by Jesus and finds Him acceptable: the story of the Woman of Samaria.

VERSE 7

One of the first "brides," a member of the church to be, is this down to earth Samaritan, now living with her sixth man. The acceptance and response of such a person, her infectious enthusiasm that generates more to turn and believe, shame many church members whose outlook is more like the elder brother in the Prodigal Son. The discourse itself takes us into a recurrent theme of John's, that of Jesus as the water of life. Here is living water, the water that gives eternal life. The water that not only washes and cleanses, but also sustains life. More than sustaining the unborn child and carrying it into the world on the flood as the waters break, if we pick up the imagery of the dialogue with Nicodemus, here is water to sustain us and carry us through and beyond our life. As water is to the oasis, so Jesus is to us. No wonder the woman thought her labors were over! (v.15; 4:14; 7:35; Isa 55:1–2).

VERSES 22–23

It is significant that the Greek work for worship in these verses and verse 24 can also mean "come to kiss." It not only suggests our approach to the Christ child but the irony of Judas' betrayal.

VERSE 24

We have that lovely revelation of worship: God is spirit, and those who worship Him must worship in spirit and in truth. The kingdom is not confined to Jerusalem but to wherever we worship and acknowledge God.

As the dialogue continues (v.26) Jesus reveals himself as the Christ, the Messiah (literally the Anointed One). This is not something Jesus does as a matter of course. It fits in with our seeing Him as the groom, but during His lifetime He was very cagey about whom He told. Rather, the work of God is that people should turn and believe in Him (6:29). Again in the absence of any scene of transfiguration and Peter's confession and admonition, Jesus' glory is evidenced in the raising of Lazarus and the recognition of Him as Christ by Martha in response to Jesus: "I am the resurrection and the life" (11:21–27).

VERSES 31–38

In the aside to the disciples on the harvest being ready and they enter into reaping what they did not sow, Jesus is the seed, the Word, in the sense of the parable of the sower which all the synoptic gospels include (Matt 13:1–9; Mark 4:1–9; Luke 8:4–8). Again the work of the groom is to initiate the labor in which the whole church is involved.

In the end Jesus' time in Samaria bears much fruit, and they acknowledge Him as Savior of the World (v.42). Ironically, two verses later Jesus acknowledges that a prophet has no honor at home, but there seems to have been some respite amongst those who had been up at the feast in Jerusalem with Him.

Chapter 4 closes with a description of Jesus' second sign, the healing of the son of the official at Capernaum. Perhaps this can be paralleled by some of the healings recounted in the other gospels—the ruler of the Synagogue or the centurion at Capernaum. Capernaum is an interesting and reasonably large town to visit, commanding the north end of the Sea of Galilee and the crossing of the river to the north. The crusaders built a later town below the source of the Jordan at Baneas which served the commanding site of Nimrod castle to the north east.

It is also interesting to note that Jesus is fairly cynical about those who approach Him out of the blue: "Unless you see signs and wonders you will not believe." But on receiving some assurance, the real mark of Jesus the man is His compassion, an unconditional love of all people whatever their circumstances. Only their response to Him can unlock His love and open a channel of grace. So again in the second sign there is more proof of the nature of the bridegroom.

Chapter 5

SOME SOURCES SAY CHAPTER 6 should follow chapter 4, but when 4:45 mentions that Jesus had done something at the feast it must refer to 2:13 or 4:45 and the Passover feast when Jesus cleansed the temple. It must be sufficient to take the text as we find it, so there is no harm in that the train of thought moves on to another feast in chapter 5, rather than a walk-about around the Sea of Galilee in chapter 6.

So while the second sign was about restoring a child to health, it again makes the point that they are not excluded but very welcome. Perhaps something we should think about in the Anglican communion, when it comes to comparing notes with the other denominations, on first communion, or on sharing some bread at the altar rail before confirmation. In the case of children it is a step along the way when they are impressionable about being included. The third sign is about making the invalid walk.

Again Jesus stirs up controversy by His action. In healing the man He tells him to pick up his bed and walk, in direct contravention of the Sabbath and, in the words of the argument that follows, declares that God is working still. His further meeting with Jesus (5:14) produces another comment on the matter: "See, you are well! Sin no more that nothing worse befall you." Now to the Jews the man was already sinning (literally, falling short) in failing to obey their commandments over the Sabbath! Sin and illness were seen as linked but this invalid could not get into the water quickly enough. Creation has to continue as it was there before the commandments were given. So again the power and the position of the groom and his relation to the Father is manifest. This further fuels hatred of the Jews against Jesus (v.18).

VERSE 18

Jesus' actions and claims raised a challenge and marked out a thin dividing line between belief and unbelief. At the same time it linked faith into the concept that creation continued and mankind did not mark time until the final day of judgment before entering into God's continuing work. Calling God "Father" made Jesus equal with God. In the sense that someone like Alexander the Great cultivated his own divinity, there are parallels to be seen. Alexander achieved much more than the conquest of the known world for he actually enabled rule to continue. For this achievement alone he was deified, rather as predecessor Darius III was considered a god. Beyond this though it was felt that to worship Alexander was to seek benefits from him in what he might bestow in states or cities. Further to this still he had absolute power. Now Jesus had the achievements in what He did and taught. He had the compassion which offered benefits. The sum of all this was the power, but power He was not prepared to use to become a temporal king (see 6:15). So as the bridegroom's glory grows, as the Son of the Father begins to be more clearly seen, Jesus has to fill out the picture. His earthly rule shows. He brings life and restores life. That is what makes Him so attractive.

VERSE 25

So the Father loves the Son and shows the Son His work. The Son follows in the same mold as any other son follows up His father's work and walks in His shoes. As the Father raises the dead and gives them life, so too the Son has the same power and freedom, which is illustrated in chapter 11. However, the Father delegates judgment to the Son so the Son can enjoy honor as the Father does. Here the power of Jesus exceeds that of the other temporal monarchs, whether they claim divinity or not, for to hear Jesus and believe Him to be sent by God was to have eternal life, and in enjoying this life to bypass judgment and death. The old emperors could not avoid the grave and maybe were worshiped beyond the grave (nine hundred years in the case of Alexander in Egypt) but their power ended there. Here is something that is not cut short by death but triumphs over it and raises us to new life beyond.

So the Son of God, executor of Judgment, calls us to life. To hear His voice is to live. The enigma of the title "Son of Man" occurs here and in this context is perhaps closest to having an explanation. Here is a title that Jesus uses of himself to explain the nature and role of the groom. This is different from the Son of Man who must be lifted up (3:14), as Moses lifted up the serpent in the wilderness for healing those who looked to it (Num 21:9 and also the R.A.M.C.[1] cap badge). In John's gospel the title does not refer to Jesus as I or me but more specifically to judgment or healing. Certainly Dan 7:13 is not without influence and being part of a traditional corpus of literature during the inter-testament times, the idiom would still have been fairly fresh. Perhaps it carries its own irony in that before He is glorified and recognized as the Son of God He must endure human suffering at human hands in its vilest form, and not only be subject to man but to serve Him as well. However faintly we may comprehend the title and whatever else we may read into it, whether from scholars or humble ordinands writing their essays, here is the Lord of resurrection. There are two paths ahead. For those who do good, resurrection to life. For those who do bad, resurrection to judgment.

VERSE 30

On judgment Jesus has more to say. It is not His will but God's and His decision is based on what He hears. So here is the culmination of the evidence of the identity of the groom. It is not sufficient to

1. RAMC stands for Royal Army Medical Corps whose cap badge is the Serpent on Moses' pole.

blow His own trumpet: the evidence of more witnesses is required. There is John, the primary witness to the light, but there is also the evidence of the deeds themselves for they point to the divine power. Jesus then goes on to suggest that if His word took root in those who confront Him and who criticize or condemn Him, they too would be His witnesses, but the Word is not in them. Where the Word rests, there the Word speaks. So if God is not with them, they search in vain. Even the scriptures they overlook, though they point to Him and in Him there is the eternal life they seek. The scriptures and Moses are His secondary witnesses. Here is a major clash between what is of God and what is of men. Nicodemus was refuted by the Sanhedrin. Gamaliel fared better and got them to listen and weigh things up (7:50). Nicodemus urged them to hear and learn what He did before making judgment. Gamaliel's warning is that if the new teaching is of men it will fail, but if of God then they are in danger of opposing God (Acts 5:34).

While they basked in the glory they gave each other they missed out on the glory that comes from God. Man blinded by his own dim radiance! The more obvious liar or charlatan they will receive, but not one who claims no glory from men but manifests the glory of God. The rejection that ends in the cross already has its roots here! So Jesus is not going to whinge to the Father and issue counter accusations. They look to Moses, and Moses foretold Jesus. As they won't accept that evidence then it will be Moses who is their accuser (Deut 18:15–22). As what Jesus says comes to pass, His word is true and is therefore what God gave Him to say. The emphasis is clearly on the identity of the groom as the pre-existent Word of God. Grooms who center the marriage day on themselves rather than the bride do not enjoy a long marriage.

It would be interesting to consider at this point what of the Old Testament does point to Jesus, the Messiah. This may be more along the lines of what Matthew includes in his gospel as fulfillment or a rule of thumb through the scriptures along the lines of Luke 24:27: "when beginning with Moses and the prophets, He interpreted to them in all the scriptures the things concerning himself."

Gen 3:15:	The Serpent cursed.
Gen 22:18	Promise to Abraham etc. Isaac considered raised from the dead when spared as a sacrifice because God provided.
Num 21:9	Bronze serpent to heal from the cross.
Deut 18:15	Moses on the Messiah and false prophets.
Ps 16:9,10	Resurrection.
Ps 22:14–17	Looking on the wounds of Him they have pierced.
Zech 12:10, 13:6	As above.
Ps 69:21	Vinegar to drink.
Ps 107	Jesus calms the storm: Son of Man title given to those redeemed and delivered (Judgment).
Ps 132:4	Promise to David of a successor.
Isa 7:14	A young woman shall conceive and bear a son.
Isa 9:6	Son is born, prince of peace.
Isa 40:10–11	Voice in the wilderness, prepare the way of the Lord. John the Baptist.
Isa 50:6	I gave my back to the smiters: Crucifixion.
Isa 53	He was wounded for their transgressions.
Jer 23:5	A righteous branch raised up for David.
Jer 33:14,15	Fulfill promise to Israel. 31:31: a new covenant.
Ezek 34:23	I will set over them one shepherd.
Ezek 37:29	My dwelling place shall be in their midst: open sanctuary/one covenant.
Dan 9:24	A time to atone for iniquity: seal vision and prophecy; anoint Holy place.
Mic 7:20	Promise to Abraham fulfilled.
Mal 3:1	A messenger of a new covenant sent.
Mal 4:2	Son of righteousness will arise with healing in His wings.

Chapter 6

THE FEEDING OF THE five thousand occurs in all four gospels (Matt 14:13–21; Mark 6:30–44; Luke 9:10–17). It must have been a momentous occasion. Matthew and Mark must have their own reasons for making a further comparison when four thousand are fed (Matt 15:32–39; Mark 8:1–9). If we follow the theme of Jesus as the groom through John's gospel, here is a very important landmark for Jesus in the provider of bread. His own commentary follows and links into the whole consideration of the sacraments at the communion table.

It is close to the Passover, which gives us a time and an occasion. The two named players are Philip (might he have been a baker?) and Andrew, both of whom in the first chapter recognized Jesus when He was pointed out and went out to find someone else and share the good news. A third player is a young lad with five barley loaves and two fish, either a good boy scout or rather like the young David running errands to those doing men's work. In fact it is the men who sat down and numbered five thousand. There may have been more people besides but John leaves us in no doubt that after Jesus gave thanks they all ate their fill from the original provisions, held by the lad. This is the fourth sign and worthy of manifesting Jesus as a prophet.

Some like to think of it as mini first Eucharist, others that each had and shared their own allowances. In fact it poses more questions than we can answer, however pragmatic our outlook may be. Fish feature prominently in the gospel and regularly are part of any fast shared, yet today do not feature at all except as traditional fare on Fridays and in the form of the acrostic and symbol ICHTHUS: Jesus Christ, Son of God, Savior. Imagine communion including a morsel of kipper![1]

VERSE 15

Such power and provision proved attractive to all the people. Here was a suitable King. Jesus beat a hasty retreat!

VERSES 16–21

Then follows the most amazing incident, which describes the very heart of baptism if we focus on some of the words. For in the act of being at sea in a storm there is a parallel with ourselves being adrift in our lives when "Jesus had not yet come to them" (v.17). In the turmoil they took Him on board (v.21). In other words, on accepting Him and taking Him on board, they arrived. Four miles puts them a long way for Capernaum: the Sea of Galilee is not all that wide. It is certainly prone to strong winds tearing up or down the valley all of a sudden. It is the head of the Rift Valley that stretches all the way down to Lake Victoria in Africa. At Tiberias there used to be an amusing notice, "Beware of western wimps suddenly sweeping," on the shore to the north of the town, near the Scottish Hospice.

"It is I; do not be afraid." If there is any form of second Advent, is not this it? When we as individuals take Jesus on board for who He is, there is no need for further fear and He then comes to the individual. Thus any second coming after the resurrection and ascension can be seen as a staggered continuous event dependent on the individual's response.

1. The fish symbol ◯< was also a means by which Christians recognized each other during times of persecution. When greeting each other they described semi-circles in the dust with their feet to overlap and form the symbol.

Finally, compare these verses with Ps 107:23–32: verse 28, "They cried to the Lord in their distress" and verse 30, "Then they were glad because they are at rest. . . and he brought them to their desired haven." Such are His works to the sons of men! Again the thought is there, that all are sons of men. Do not overlook the background influence of the psalms for they would have been known by heart. God stirs up and brings calm. In the chaos at the beginning there is the Spirit of disturbance, now the comforter through Christ.

VERSES 22–40: THE BREAD OF LIFE

First of all it starts with a boat chase as the people seek Jesus after He had given them the bread, on giving thanks. On catching up with Him there is a lively debate on physical and spiritual food: food which perishes and only feeds the body, or food that endures and raises up to eternal life when the Son of Man distributes himself.

Again as a sign, the feeding of so many shows on whom God has set His seal. They are drawn further: "What must we do to be doing the works of God?" (v.28). The reply, merely to believe in the one He has sent, despite the signs they have seen is not enough. "What sign do you do?" etc. Here is something better than manna direct from heaven, able to give life to the world. They want nothing better for evermore! (v.34). Like the woman of Samaria who thought she would be spared fetching more water, they anticipated a Utopia at face value of magic bread. Ps 107:33–38 talks of God blessing the earth and feeding the hungry. Ps verse 43 ends on a note of wise reflection.

In the explanation that follows, our groom is the bread of life. To come to Him is to hunger no more for He provides the bread; to believe in Him is never to thirst again. So in the background there are twelve baskets of bread that have been collected up, that nothing that God has given Him is wasted (v.39). We might also call to mind all the water turned into wine at the wedding that obviously was not wasted either! So what the Father gives the Son is not to be rejected. The Son is obedient to the Father and will raise it up at the last day. This suggests an offering that is given to the Almighty and so it is: all who see and believe the Son will have eternal life. Furthermore God's provision is always plentiful.

VERSES 41–49

This obviously causes some dispute. They know His parents so how can He come down from heaven? Again further explanation helps and throws light on the perspective that the Father must prompt people towards the Son. This is the hidden work of the Spirit. God himself teaches people. To come from God is to have seen Him and therefore be very able to offer eternal life. Then the shell bursts (v.51): "and the bread which I give for the life of the world is my flesh." Here we really enter into the meaning of the sacraments, anticipating the sacrifice on the cross. It is a relationship sealed in the flesh, like the consummation of a marriage, and sealed with a cup. The vessel containing the wine will be broken so again there is the sacrifice; the glass and its shattering just as it takes place at a wedding. To take Jesus on board in the bread and the wine, in the sacraments suggesting flesh and blood, is to have Jesus abiding within us and us in Him. Again the consummation of the union of groom and bride, Christ and His church, us, and the consecration of it all is explained. As in Genesis the divided Adam is made one with Eve in marriage, so Jesus, made our flesh but divided in death, becomes one with us again through the bread and wine of communion. We are the new vehicle, His body.

VERSES 60–65

Well, this was hard for them to stomach! But the explanation is spiritual as much as physical when we look back after the event. The clock does not go back. The Son of Man moves on and creation continues. The Spirit gives life, the flesh is merely a mortal vehicle. These words, rehearsed at each communion service are spirit and life. Yet behind it there is still the pull of the prompting of the Father. Yet even at the altar rail there are those who betray Him.

VERSES 66–END

Twice within seven verses there is mention of a betrayer known to Jesus. Peter acknowledges Jesus as the Holy One of God, and accepts it all: "You have the words of eternal life." All are chosen by Jesus to play their respective parts in His life and earthly work. For the Father to draw someone to Him, that person had to be open to the work of the Spirit, sometimes acting like a real nutcracker! Judas remained closed.

Chapter 7

VERSES 2,37

The Feast of Tabernacles is one of the three great Jewish Festivals, along with Passover (passing over and sparing the Israelites before the Exodus) and Pentecost (fifty days: Feast of the First Fruits). It was the feast of the ingathering at the end of the year—harvest home (Exod 23:14–16). It lasted seven days and was followed by an eighth day of Holy Convocation (what psalms might you identify as being used?). During the feast the people lived in booths and even today these can be seen on the rooftops where palm leaves etc. are laid across a framework. This commemorates ancient Israel's sojourn in the wilderness (Lev 23:34ff, 39ff; Neh 8:4ff). Some of the ceremonial surrounding the occasion included the use of lights and libations or water (the bronze sea would be filled in the temple).

It is no small wonder that Jesus, considering all the effort that went into getting precious water to the temple and storing it there, should refer to himself as living water and echo Ezek 47:9–10. (Everywhere the river flowed from the temple, it would bring life).

Under pressure from His brothers to reveal himself and prove himself, Jesus makes much the same reply to them as to His mother at Cana (v.6): "My time has not yet come." So again the groom causes consternation, yet for a little while He remains in secret and private. When He did go up halfway through the festivities and began to teach, He caused further amazement: where did His learning come from as He had never studied? Again Jesus gives God the credit, and refuses to seek His own glory which indeed is one of the temptations open to Him, although John does not mention forty days in the wilderness and three temptations like the synoptic gospels.

He does, however, remind them of deeds that bear Him witness and the controversy that that caused. Yet to obey Moses' law they circumcise on the Sabbath to complete things, so to speak, but are not prepared to accept someone being made whole on the Sabbath that he in turn may keep it better as well! So much for keeping up appearances. Jesus wants them to exercise right judgment and be realistic.

Again (v.30) Jesus' hour had not come so He was not arrested. People still had difficulty identifying him as the Messiah, despite John's testimony and the measure of the signs performed so far. Rather like children with a conjurer, they always want more! Enigmatically, Jesus point to a little while more then being out of reach, or a little while more and they will not want to be where He is. So on the last day of the feast Jesus makes His announcement and identifies himself as the living water. When He is glorified then the Spirit will be poured out. We must, however, keep in mind the baptism with water on which this idea builds.

VERSES 40–END

Some, of course, begin to recognize Jesus for who He is. The prophet. The Christ. John tells us nothing of Jesus' roots nor includes a nativity story. In His lifetime Jesus was recognized as a Galilean. Few would think where He was born, but John mentions the scripture in passing, for those who want to or need to know. The only equivalent interest in where someone was born used to be the Yorkshire County Cricket Club! More evidence of the character and background of the groom is here. Arrest proves impossible, but John has no qualms in underlining the contempt of the priests for the people. A change of air is overdue! The contrast to the regimentation of the law and the ignorance of the people is reflected in the authority of Jesus' teaching whose source the Pharisees cannot accept. Even Nicodemus is sent packing in their frustration. They won't hear him and they'll only take from scripture what suits them.

Chapter 8

VERSES 1–11

Probably the biggest threat to any marriage is adultery. It is number six on the list of ten commandments. It is forgivable. It is also the most commonly used idiom in the Old Testament describing any breach of relationship and covenant between God and Israel (man). It focuses our attention on the groom and becomes a very subjective insight into the special relationship we see through St. John's gospel.

Here is forgiveness in action and a portrait of the Son of God to whom authority to execute judgment has been given (John 5:27). But again we must consider what an accurate reflection on human nature the incident is, and a clear condemnation of our own behavior.

All too often, when a marriage does hit hard times and the marriage bed is violated it is pride rather than a lack of forgiveness that prevents reconciliation. However, if we consider the covenant relationship and its attendant blessings and curses, it is obvious that a broken marriage rapidly becomes a curse round both partners' necks, unless they are prepared to forgive. How the church cultivates a forgiving face and treads the knife edge between maintaining the sanctity of marriage and moral standards, and practicing forgiveness, is extremely delicate. In any event no subsequent relationship stands much chance if there is not forgiveness of the first. Is not forgiveness an aspect of love in action whereby a previous marriage vow is maintained, in a sense, rather than broken? This, perhaps, is the way forward out of this very human dilemma that we should consider, and its foundations are clearly rooted here if we apply the permutations of forgiveness to the situation. The woman taken in adultery can also be seen in us, the bride, the church, being forgiven if we fall away no more.

VERSES 12–20

Jesus is the Light of the World. Not only is the nature of Jesus clearly revealed in the previous incident over the woman caught in adultery (though one wants to ask the question, where is the bloke or what became of him?), but Jesus is tackled once again by the Pharisees over witnesses to His identity. Obviously they judge according to the flesh, not only Him, but the woman they marched in front of Him. The incident itself conjures up ghoulish pictures of degenerates lying in wait for her, rather like the story of Susanna and the elders! Again Jesus points to the Father. To know the Son is to know the Father. The bridegroom's credentials are impeccable but still there are those who are too stiff necked to accept him. It is a further hint of John's mysterious conclusion that Jesus' hour has not yet come.

VERSES 21–30

Judgment continues to exist here and now and not at the last day. It boils down simply to acceptance or rejection of Jesus as the Son. The nature of darkness is the rejection of God and being lost in one's own sins. Christ is above and those who accept Him are with Him. To be lifted up is not only to be enjoined to the Father again but hints at the crucifixion and salvation in the manner of Moses' bronze serpent. Light and life: seeing life in the light of Jesus, or in the case of Lazarus to have life in Jesus literally, reflects something of the psalms: "In thy light may we see light" (Ps 36:9, and Job 33:28,30).[1]

1. Hanson, *Prophetic Gospel*, 117ff.

VERSES 31–59

Pilate later asks, "What is truth?" (18:38). The truth brings freedom and lies in our being Jesus' disciple and continuing in His word. At the very start of his gospel, John launches out into the realm of grace and truth (1:18). Grace is God's forgiveness by taking the burden of our sin on Himself on the cross. The truth is there for those who will accept it. Discussion on freedom, seen in terms of God's ancient promise to Abraham, follows. Slavery to sin is well aired by Paul in his letter to the Romans (6:16). They cannot grasp that what comes directly from God the Father substitutes first place for any previous promises to the forefathers. Again debate rages over fatherhood. Sons of God or Sons of Abraham? Divine or mortal? Raised up or reduced by our baser nature? Higher achievements or reduced to works of the devil and his desires? To really hear, one must be of God. A suggestion is that unless God attracts us, the Spirit does not work in us. This is much the same chemistry as boy meets girl and the relationship deepens from there. Verse 44: Evil exists through choice: they are of the Devil because they make the wrong choice.

Because Jesus doesn't conform, the Jews accuse Him of being a Samaritan. Again He stresses the witness to himself by the Father. The Jews try to accuse Him of having a demon in reply to His saying they are of the devil previously. Again it is implied that those who accept Him will become His witnesses too. Jesus tries to argue His precedence to Abraham to get them on the right track but His words are turned against Him. They cannot accept that as Son of God He must have pre-existence with God long before Abraham! He dodges out of range and out of sight, but certainly not out of mind.[2] Paul in chapter 4 of his letter to the Romans has to tackle the same debate to explain himself: "All I know is I was blind, now I can see" (John 9:25).

2. v.57. This prompts a debate on Jesus' age. If we take the date of the star at His birth as Halley's comet of 12BC, it would make Jesus about 45 in AD 33 at the time of His crucifixion. Not yet 50 but not far off it!

Chapter 8

VERSE 39: JUDGMENT

Compare Isaiah's second sermon (chapter 29): the doom of blind hypocrites.

Chapter 9

SEEING IS BELIEVING

JESUS' HEALINGS RESTORE AND enhance life but they do not avert disasters. The synoptic temptations clearly identify that Jesus will accept life as it is and not change the laws of nature. That does put stilling the storm in a particular light, but then any healing does along with the raising of Lazarus. Alongside that is the symbolic meaning behind all the healings: blind, deaf, lame, dead. We need to understand Jesus, be alive to Him and walk in His way.

The next sign is healing the man born blind so that he may see and recognize Jesus. It borders on the farce as the authorities fail to accept the obvious and send for the bloke's parents. Sin and illness were seen in a very different light two thousand years ago from this day and age. Perhaps we lose out, for illness when it is dis-ease may well have the same roots and healing only may come when wholeness is restored. This can be inclined towards too much jargon for many to understand easily, but the simplicity of the disease being countered by wholeness must be obvious enough. The biggest problem facing the healing ministry is those persons who lift the first century Jesus out of the context of His life and times and plop Him down in the twentieth century. Fundamentalism and naivety go hand in hand here. We cannot demand miracles of God. Yet within our own makeup we contain many trigger mechanisms to counteract the problem if they can be set off. It comes with peace of mind.

The questions the disciples raise would be on the lips of many. In the light of ancient understanding, who had sinned?[1] The man, or his parents, in that he was born blind? The Old Testament God of wrath and punishment, like a prep school headmaster, is in the background. Instead Jesus breaks through a barrier, as much mental blockage and conditioning of the day, to present a New Testament God of compassion and response. The work of God is known no more as punishment but healing, wholeness, restoration, mercy, love, forgiveness and completeness. We may still ask what sort of God can allow mass starvation, epidemics, floods and subsequent disasters, AIDS and thalidomide casualties, but are we asking the right question? Man has free will within which restriction God works, if it is a restriction to Him. More it is that He knows us inside out, rather like parents knowing their children, so He knows what choices we will make before we make them. Thus many of the problems that cause much heart searching are the results of our own actions: greed, power struggles (have any of the African countries lived through their middle ages like Europe?) and selfishness. Much of aid is now aimed at education and self-help, clean water, better drainage and less abuse of water sources; engineering aims to help areas subject to frequent floods, because the fertility of delta areas means there is a living to be made for many that would be impossible further inland; our own sexual excesses and vanity and greed to make money out of drugs must be the main reason behind the last group of problems, not the hand of God. However, we must not let a rather glib global rationale cloud our compassion for anyone struck down by disaster. Civil war in Syria, and Gaza now, is more difficult to alleviate, especially when civilians and food for them are either hostages or bargaining chips. It is worth noting that Jesus came to restore our humanity, not religion; our faith, not an empty ritual. It was the Pharisees

1. The concept of sin as "falling short" is based on a word picture illustrating firing an arrow at a target, and sinning = falling short. Not for nothing did the Cavalry and Infantry nickname the Artillery, being behind the front line, "Drop short" if it landed shells on them!

with three books of man-made laws who had hedged in God and the Ten Commandments, making life difficult.

It does remind us of chapter 6:15, "perceiving that they were about to come and take Him by force to make Him king": that many of man's problems are the result of his own understanding and action in a situation. Many in Jesus' day expected the Messiah to be a triumphant warrior who would throw off the Roman yoke, restore Israel and Judah, and rule like David. Today we see power struggles come to blows and force used to impose one way on those with other ideas. In Europe old feuds continue and in Africa tribal hostility, similar to anything prior to our own middle ages, becomes civil war. Despite having a United Nations force, nothing can be achieved where there is no will for peace, to say nothing of the corruption that exists within the UN. Despite the best motives aid gets into the wrong hands, becomes currency and prolongs the struggle. Would not a better approach be found, and be a better channel of compassion, if the rival forces were left to fight it out and settle it first, and then aid was sent in? Such was T.E. Lawrence's verdict on Arab problems. There is some hope that those who fled may be able to renegotiate their property, but once a cross section of people are dependent on a third party, as Trump would have Gaza and Ukraine surrender to his dictation, they no longer have any hope of swaying the balance. Furthermore, when aid is sent in you never see starving soldiers or terrorists. Those with the guns take what they want first. Syria, Gaza, and Yemen are both at an impasse as I write.

So Jesus manifests the works of God and heals the blind man, having made a form of salve. On further investigation the deed causes uproar! Ironically the impact of Jesus is clouded by preconceptions of God and the keeping of the Sabbath, even though the deeds begin to speak for themselves and witness to Jesus being from God. As I tried to explain previously, here is an example of Jesus not fitting a context in His own time, just as now we try and fit Him to our own contemporary context, only to find it does not work. We need to grasp the message from John about Jesus being the way, the truth and the life, the ultimate Word from God and work Him into our everyday. Hopefully there is no penalty for confessing Jesus to be Christ as there was in 9:22!

In passing, it is interesting to note from the gospels that where Jesus heals adults they are told to go and do something—wash, show yourself to the priests, don't follow me and tell the folks here, sin no more, etc. When it comes to children, they are restored to their parents who are told to give them something to eat. If taken merely on an allegorical level, what does it tell us about bringing our own children to faith? If old enough, of an age to be asked, they obviously answer for themselves. We need to make it as plain but as attractive as possible for them to do so. Even so, any C.U. will win some and lose some if it is the only channel of contact. For younger persons, how we feed them (and this anticipates Jesus' command to Peter in John 21:15–"Feed my lambs") and the nurturing demands more responsibility. Merely receiving bread at communion along with a blessing may help towards participating in and respecting the sacraments later on. As dialogue and discussion are more difficult until a person is older, should not confirmation and the age of consent go hand in hand so that other values are brought in when the individuals have to find out how much value they put on themselves and their own bodies too? Much can only be done by example and living out the faith. However, if Christianity is to have any input, it must relate to a knowledge of the scriptures, the stories and the teaching of Jesus. And how to handle them. Baptism and confirmation have become divorced; we need to bridge the gap! If we baptize infants then it needs serious follow-up in later years, so maybe it should be aimed more at adults.

VERSES 24F

We now reach a point where the recipient of Jesus' love and healing power begins to witness to Him. It is not a bed of roses! First the deed itself speaks: "though I was blind, now I see." Secondly His simple logic tells them God does not listen to sinners, so to cure the blind He must be from God. Thirdly it implies that while the authorities are still stuck on the Mosaic law and being disciples of Moses, others have moved on as the world around them opens up. He is condemned as a sinner and rejected. The mere fact of healing has removed any condemnation of sin, if it ever existed. Mercifully the human being is such that what the person does not know otherwise poses no problem. Rather the person lives with and through the circumstances in which they find themselves. So when the world opens up, the person does not dwell on the past and its improbabilities and imponderables but looks ahead. As we are told, the woman rejoices after childbirth over the child born and does not dwell on the pain of childbirth.

VERSE 35

Now when Jesus sounds him out it is interesting that his reaction to hearing about the Son of Man is to want to believe in Him. This suggests the title carried its own preset expectations and description. The enigma is for those who do not see Him or recognize Him or respond to Him. In return, those who remain blind become guilty of the sin they would impute on others.

Chapter 10

So Jesus enters into a description in almost the same breath of himself as the good shepherd. This should ring a few bells from the Old Testament so that the number of witnesses to Him may increase historically and practically.

THE GOOD SHEPHERD

Here the groom describes his job in an allegory that draws heavily on the Old Testament for its imagery. Here is the true shepherd of the sheep foretold by Ezek 34:11. Previously the sheep have been devoured by their own shepherds, but now a new regime begins. It is a contrast to Luke, where real shepherds are drawn to the birth of the infant Jesus and wonder at the sign they are given and receive because the Lord God promises to be the shepherd: here the Son keeps the promise. Again His work becomes His testimony to His identity. But also, the sheep without a proper caring shepherd have soiled their own situation (Ezek 34:18). Their new shepherd, the good shepherd, is the new David (v.23). Alongside this can be counted the myriad of other prophesies concerning the root or stump of Jesse, especially Isaiah and Zech 12–13, which finishes with the fate of the shepherd (Zech 13:7) and is echoed in Matt 26:31, which prompted the prophecy of Peter's denial.

The only time I see sheep following a shepherd in England is when the farmer has ewes in lamb that need to be moved to new pasture. By waving a bag, which they think is feed, they will follow. Otherwise I've only seen sheep follow their shepherd in hotter climates, especially the Holy Land. In Germany I have seen the shepherd dog (Alsatian) doing his proper work, but for the most part here the farmers keep an old coat that they always wear because the sheep know it and will follow him. They use sheep dogs for rounding up sheep when they are more scattered.

VERSE 7

Jesus is also the door. Thoroughfare is through Him only. Salvation is equated with safety, and the comparison of the failures of Ezekiel's description with thieves is accurate; an abundance of full life is the object of the good shepherd. Success is built on mutual knowledge and trust, which stems from the Father. Further testimony: like Father, like Son, to add to the witness of those who do accept. The job, however, is dangerous and there is a penalty: He lays his life down for the sheep (v.15, elaborated in chapter 15:13).

It is in this sentiment of "Greater love has no man than that he lay down his life for his friends" that is the backbone of middle class Anglicanism. The whole ethos of Remembrance Sunday is centered on this as the supreme sacrifice. Through the loss of friends and colleagues in a steady stream of six wars this century and attendant peace keeping duties (Boer War, two World Wars, Korea, Falklands, Gulf x 3, Malay, Aden, East Africa, Cyprus and Northern Ireland Emergencies), Britain has rationalized her losses. One could say that the habit of toasting R.A.F. pilots who did not return from operations in the mess that night was a sort of Eucharistic ritual of farewell and memorial. See various authors on the subject: Hill and Johnson who wrote of it, and particularly about Mick Mannock, a WWI ace who keened in this way when his fellow pilots were lost. They are seen as a practical expression of faith and moral values. Being left with hardly any standing army at the end of the twentieth century is a real challenge to the future of the established church. The English tradition of spirituality nurtured on sacrifice drew heavily on being nourished through the services and the empire. Given a generation that does not know sacrifice in such stark terms based on a training to serve others, or until the end of the 1950s on National Service, the Church of England is going to have to teach from a very different perspective. The good news is that the charitable response of the nation is not just humanism and many young, conscious of being given so much, want to put something back into society. In that sense the church begins to shape its own message as expression is found through contemporary avenues.

VERSES 16 AND 17

In gathering the flock into one fold and uniting this church (and I write this particular paragraph during the week of prayer for Christian unity!) the shepherd has a full schedule ahead for some time. The suggestion here is that the work goes beyond the resurrection but that the resurrection is part of it.

It is the free will given to us by God that must be behind Jesus' power to lay down His life and take it up again. Verse 18: it lies in His obedient response to the Father as to how the Father responds in turn. The implications are beyond those who do not want to accept what Jesus says. The usual furor results, but it poses the question on the lips on many so far: can a man with a demon open the eyes of the blind? Ironically he cannot, certainly not the eyes of those who do not want to see, but he has Holy Spirit, not a demon, that makes sight restoration possible.

VERSE 22

Yet another feast takes place, which demands a fresh orientation towards Christ. There is further irony in that it marked an earlier turning point in the life of the temple, following its desecration in 168BC by Antiochus Epiphanes, a descendant of one of Alexander's generals who divided his empire amongst themselves. When Judas Maccabeus recaptured Jerusalem he had the temple cleansed. The stones were carted away from Jerusalem. Small wonder that Herod built a temple to please the Jews. (Stones from Queen Helena's vast church were also removed as being defiled.) Mark refers to the "abomination which makes desolate" (13:14): see also Dan 11:31 which refers to this earlier desecration and which dates the second half of Daniel. This feast commemorated the rededication of the temple and makes a stand by Judaism against encroaching Hellenism in their faith and culture and daily life. There followed the Hasmonean dynasty, which Herod the Great eventually usurped, causing its last survivor to be drowned in the swimming pool of his palace just up the road from Herod's lovely winter palace at Jericho with its orchards and running water, collected and piped in a culvert through the wilderness, which is still running.

Jesus repeats His explanation: what He does in God's name bears legal witness to Him. His gift of eternal life, not just food, and His oneness with the Father still fail to convince the Jews! The way John refers to the Jews suggests he wrote in the light of a definite rift between Jesus and His followers with conventional Judaism, but I would hesitate to date it to the post resurrection period of opposition, encountered and explained in the early chapters of Acts, or to later years post the destruction of Jerusalem in AD70 which marked a final severance of Christianity from Judaism, within which it had managed to exist as a charismatic movement.

Eternal life in verse 28 is literally "age lasting." It has a beginning but no end, so must be integral in the on-going nature of God. Perhaps best explained as being "of God." 1 Pet 1:5 and 1 Cor 15 expand on this theme. Suffice to say it is a spiritual, not an immortal physical, life.

Jesus finds what witnesses to Him brushed aside and He is confronted with the charge of blasphemy. A mortal cannot be Son of God in their eyes. Yet a pointer can be found in the scriptures (Ps 82:6). As God pronounces this title having taken His seat in the divine council prior to making judgment, it is a weighty word. As the authoritative word of God which Jesus accepted, they should have been able to accept and understand this interpretation, especially as Jesus orientated events and festivals around himself. It was integral to His prophetic witness. Even His plea to them to accept the works (v.38) as a pointer is rejected.

This seems to end Jesus' public ministry of teaching and events take a full circle as He ends up where John first baptized. The period calling out the witnesses ends where it first began in the first chapter. Already we see a very different interpretation of likely judgment by God (v.28 and Ps 82). It would be a good stage to pause and reflect on the nature of God before tackling the raising of Lazarus, which is His last sign and builds on the place of judgment and the nature of eternal life through the sequence of its own events. Perhaps it is the ultimate gift of the groom to bride before he gives himself, demonstrating the power he has described.

Chapter 11

IF LAZARUS (GREEK = Without help, which we all need!) had been four days in the tomb, he would have been well and truly dead, as verse 39 of chapter 11 suggests. As already explained, eternal life has to do with on-going or age lasting life, not immortality of the body, so the raising of Lazarus plays a particular part in explaining this and bridging the gap to Jesus' resurrection, which was of a different nature (chapter 20). Lazarus is raised to everyday life and restored. It is good for friends and family, even if it causes concern to the Jews. But Jesus' death and resurrection goes beyond that. This is a passing milestone of His power that is God given, as described in chapter 10. Indeed His power builds up to the grand finale in His resurrection. Raising Lazarus is great, but if that was the extent of resurrection it would not achieve a great deal if more widely available. It would cause confusion. Imagine some people alive and others alive who had been dead! But furthermore it only restores Lazarus to where he left off. He is not imbued with any great immortality, nor even experiences judgment being waived. He continues an earthly life. Jesus has to break through the barrier that separates this life from the next, a barrier that has its own nature rooted in being purely and wholly in God. If there is nothing spiritual in the body when it expires then there is nothing to restore to God. Where there has been no spiritual life and growth, there will be nothing more to return to God. Therefore death may be a full stop for some but it does not herald a new life of fiery torture. As Jesus says, what is good for nothing is thrown away. What is spirit is of God and returns to God no lessened but fuller after an active spiritual life. Resurrection opens up a new dimension.

The Greeks had Hades with its attendant tests: the Egyptian nobility had their tombs with attendant symbolic comforts. Somewhere in the middle Jesus shakes out a new look, suggesting that the inevitable judgment as perceived in Judaism takes place here and now in our response to and acceptance of Jesus and therefore of God. What sort of loving God is gently going to roast us for an age first? God is more than an authoritative parent bewigged and gowned like a peppery old judge! So there must be a different experience of heaven and hell, that of being with God or separated from Him in this life. In the life to come there is the promise of being united in Him, for which Judaism had a picture of a heavenly feast and restoration along the lines of what was ordered in the Old Testament for the twelve tribes. There is a hint of this in the synoptics (Matt 1:28, 25:31). Rather there is a spiritual return to God or nothing. If there is nothing to go back to God then it is dead, it is finished. Emptiness waits. Silence (Ps 16:30). It is earth to earth, or in the idiom of Gehenna (Matt 23:33), the municipal rubbish dump outside Jerusalem that burned all day every day which was confused with Hades (Luke 6:23, Matt 16:18). What is finished with and worth nothing is thrown away. The weeping and wailing is at the loss or waste of a product. Would we did not live in such a consumer/disposal society today! I always feel than an important part of a funeral is saying, "Thank you." The person being buried may have been an old reprobate, but if there is room to say "Thank you" then we are saying to God that this person was of value to us and touched us spiritually so please take him back.

Lazarus, Mary and Martha are well attested in the gospels and give an air of authority to the proceedings. They were well deserving of a special gift from the groom.

However, Jesus described it as an opportunity for God to demonstrate His glory, just as the other signs had built up the image (v.4). Death, sleep and Lazarus being dead become a jumble of metaphors. No wonder the disciples were confused (v.12), and that Thomas (v.16) thought it was the end and would share His death at the hands of obviously hostile Jews. We are then enlightened along with Martha on the expectations of resurrection at the last day (v.24) and the real resurrection and life in Jesus (v.25).

So Jesus talks to Martha through death, the end of human life to a life to come, a life beyond. The real revelation at this point is Martha's exclamation (v.27) that Jesus is "the Christ, the Son of God, he who is coming into the world." That is one reason why this unique and rather incomprehensible episode over Lazarus is a pointer on the way, a gift given of the power of Jesus. It was a traumatic event for everyone concerned. Many commentaries remark on Jesus' state of mind and suggest anger, that He wept from anger and frustration (v 35). How the Jews continued to misunderstand Him! They saw love of a friend turned to grief and failure of His power. The only eyes He was failing to open were theirs! (v.37).

Here in the actual action of the raising of Lazarus we have a very different approach to some of the other miracles, though it is hinted at in the questions afterwards (v.42). This sign is for proof to those standing by that the Father did send Him. If there was humor in verse 37 about who was blind, there is irony in verse 44 about who remains bound when Jesus commanded them to "Unbind him and let him go."

There are other reasons that make the raising of Lazarus an important turning point in this gospel, besides the implied transition of varying degrees of resurrection. Resurrection is to the life beyond. There are other pointers to other important facets beyond. We are halfway through the gospel and Jesus' compassion, that was the reason behind many of His miracles and healings, above all for this one, is beginning to become passion. His intensely intimate relationship with this family of three is as close as we get to any hint of the intimacy that exists between bride and groom. This set of siblings provides a good description of the relationship between Christ and His church—us. It certainly has a real poignancy when following the suggested theme of bride and groom, and the extent of gifts and love bestowed by the groom on the bride.

Another reason for the turning point being so marked is Caiaphas' prophecy. There is an irony about it, but also the Jews are mad enough to seek His death and with the life of His friend restored, Jesus' death begins to loom on the horizon. It could even be seen that Jesus has given Lazarus his own physical life. It is expedient that one man dies for the people (v.50).

VERSE 47

John must have had some access to the Sanhedrin to know what was going on amongst them. Why they were so frightened of the Romans is a mystery in relation to Jesus, except that as potential king, He posed a threat. What impact His signs had on the Romans is conjectural. They would have been as amazed and intrigued as anyone else and gone on demanding more. See comments by Pliny, Tacitus (Jew turned Roman) and Josephus (another Romanized Jew), all contemporaries. With insurrection and revolt ever likely, especially when provoked as some histories report of Pontius Pilate, the Jews did have cause to fear the Roman war machine. Perhaps as far as Caiaphas was concerned Jesus provided a convenient scapegoat. His prophecy highlights an expediency for the Jews to survive but John sees the death that is utilized as the gathering of God's children, the making of the bride.

So the chapter ends with Jesus, a wanted man, driven to the wilderness to survive. It is back to an existence like John the Baptist in company of his disciples. The Passover is at hand. It is a time of intense preparation. There is a hint, too, that the city was the spiritual wilderness. It is a sign, not an episode of self-aggrandizement to seek attention, so is a contrast to the synoptics' temptations.

BETHANY: JOHN 1:28

John's gospel tells us Bethany is beyond the Jordan where John was baptizing. Ephraim (meaning fruitful) was thirteen miles north east of Jerusalem in the wilderness (by contrast to its name!) with views down the Jordan valley.

Chapter 12

John's gospel puts Jesus cleansing the temple at its start, as if the action continues in the gospel from there, trying to point the Jews in the right direction, culminating in the public discourses in this chapter.

Jesus celebrates with His friends. It is as if the wedding feast continues. Six days before the Passover we find Him in Bethany with Lazarus and his sisters. Martha, as ever (see Luke 10:38) serves. Mary anoints Jesus. (The story is a little different in Matt 26:6–13 and Mark 14:3–9.) Verses 4–6 are a very telling portrayal of one of His supporters, Judas Iscariot. He is always discontented with events, and is fighting against life all the way. Without prayer, without Jesus, he cannot change it, try as he might. The poor are always with us, it is a fact of life and human nature. But Jesus we do not always have, until we enter a new dimensional discussion with Him through the covenant of His blood.

VERSE 9

Rentacrowd arrive to look and marvel. Here is Lazarus who had been raised from the dead. The chief priests begin to plan His end too, because they are losing many Jews to Jesus.

VERSE 12

Five days before the Passover, Jesus enters Jerusalem with the pilgrim crowds. There is a frenzy of rejoicing. Not only did Jesus fulfill scripture (Zech 9:9) by riding an ass's colt, but the crowd was in a frenzy, witnessing to Jesus on account of His raising Lazarus from the dead, to the dismay of the Pharisees.

VERSE 20

Greek Jews had come up for the feast and wanted to see Jesus too. They approach Phillip, who with Andrew often seem to be the duty ushers. "The hour has come for the Son of Man to be glorified." Jesus speaks for the last time in public. Here even Greek culture and its heritage heads towards Jesus. A culture that combined great philosophy, wisdom and the principles of the Stoics and Epicureans now leans towards Jesus. Paul was to encounter a similar openness and tentative commitment at the Areopagus (Acts 17:16–end). Christianity begins to get a pedigree!

If the grain of wheat we store or hold in our hand is to do anything, we must plant it in the ground. Paul waxes eloquent on the subject in 1 Cor 15:35–50 and talks about the second advent of Christ in his first letter to the Thessalonians. As the wheat changes to multiply, so the human to change must let go. It is a near metamorphosis. Service and life lie in following Christ.

VERSE 27

Here we have a mini-agony (Matt 26:36–46, Mark 14:32–42, Luke 22:39–46). The temptation and thought is there to avoid what lies ahead, but God's glory must come first. This is the purpose behind all that is to follow. It is almost another burning bush experience when a voice answers Jesus' "Father, glorify thy name." This complements the synoptics version of Jesus' baptism where a voice speaks (Ps 2:7): "This is my beloved Son with whom I am well pleased" (Matt 3:13–17, Mark 1:9–11, Luke 3:21–22). Jesus is authenticated once more. By now we begin to know all the credentials of the groom before he begins his own after dinner speech.

This authentication also ushers in a new age of judgment. It is worth comparing the synoptic gospel's account of Jesus reading from Isaiah in the synagogue at Nazareth when He begins His ministry (Luke 4:18–19). In quoting Isa 61:1–2, Jesus awaits the day of vengeance of the Lord. This is not part of His ministry when it comes to releasing people. It is deliverance from this fate, from God's wrath. Who is the ruler of the world? If we take a lead from Jewish mythology and Job, it would be Satan (understand, though, on the direction of God), but it is possible to take the personification of evil too far and see him as an actual presence. In our present age it could be fair to say we are the vehicle of evil just as we are the vehicle of good. We are the devil incarnate, just as we can be the personification of Christ. If we give in to our baser instincts and become totally selfish then evil rules us; God is excluded.

VERSE 31

We are evil. But given a force for good, an example, someone we can take on board through communion, we can experience salvation. We are saved. If we are saved and stick with the good, live it, accept Jesus then we are spared the judgment. So the cross draws us to Jesus. This message, this act of God, this good news is for us.

VERSE 34

The crowd are obdurate. They have been conditioned otherwise. The law teaches them something else—or rather how others interpret that law—leading them to a different conclusion. However, they do identify the Christ, the Messiah, the Anointed One, with the Son of Man, or do they? As at baptism, we are reminded that Jesus is the light of the world (v.35), so Jesus identifies himself here to them. Enjoy it. Bask in it. Become part of it. Be sons of light.

VERSE 36

No, they did not believe in Him. Jesus hides himself. Isaiah has the final word on the present situation (Isa 53:1 and 6:1,9–10). The authorities are beginning to grasp and accept His interpretation, but worldly praise kept back those who did from any commitment and open acknowledgment of Jesus as Christ. (Nicodemus in John 3; Gamaliel in Acts 5:33–42. Paul refers to Gamaliel as his teacher: Acts 22:3.)

VERSES 44–50

John summarizes. To believe in Jesus is to believe in God as God is. To see Jesus is to see God. This revelation is new light. God almost says again, "Let light dawn." Jesus is not there to judge but the yardstick lies in rejecting Him. The Word that John describes from the beginning stands for ever; it is eternal; it is life. To reject it is to embrace death and bring judgment on oneself by one's own self. This is His gift to His bride, to us He gives His whole self and an holy inheritance. In the words of Cranmer's service of holy matrimony, the groom with his body worships or honors the bride.

Chapter 13

VERSES 1–20

I HAVE OFTEN USED these verses as a study for junior or probationary army officers. Here we find the essence of leadership. It is not the stars on the epaulets, but the ability to serve others and put them first. Then lead by example. Value other people and they will respond. See to their needs and they will do what you ask. The heart of it is humility and here the groom proves his humility. Care comes before command, expecting nothing one would not do oneself.

The hour of consummation of the relationship approaches, but first the groom illustrates the loving and cherishing of us, his bride, his church.

Judas Iscariot, son of Simon, is not content. He must work out his purpose his way. God will work His creativity through Judas and betrayal. Mankind has freewill that God has to use and work with. Jesus' washing could not cleanse Judas. He was apart. Later we see how difficult Peter found it to remain part of Jesus (vv.36–38; 18:15–18; 21:15–23).

Only love can take us beyond ourselves to God. Jesus goes on to explain that it also shows He is not greater than God but is obedient to Him. It goes a long way to explain the rather enigmatic, or for some, unpalatable, relationship that Paul describes within marriage: "wives be subject to your husbands, as to the Lord" (Eph 5:22–33). Rather, it is working together. "Behind every good man there is a woman," goes the old saying. Now we are in the twenty-first century, where do we stand when many of the women are in front of their men, or free to pick and choose as they please? Ps 41: even the old, established rules of fellowship will be broken, making the betrayal a very low act indeed, but also, if we take the commentary from Paul in 1 Cor 11:23–24, a point at which we call judgment on ourselves.

VERSES 21–30

Judas had been included amongst those washed, but he cannot enter into that interdependency that Jesus outlines. It is well described by Stephen Verney in chapter 5 of his book *Into The New Age*,[1] and he puts it into the context of grace within his own marriage experience. Grace is beyond Judas, so is the declension: "I AM, THOU ART, HE IS." Even the cross with its three dimensions echoes it: I AM like a man standing firm on the ground; THOU ART as He opens and outstretches His arms towards others: HE IS as He points to the sky. Note that in some of his sculptures of the crucifix, Eric Gill carves Jesus with His right hand, though nailed to the cross, raised in a sign of blessing.

Perhaps death on a cross begins here with a broken heart—Jesus was troubled in spirit. Betrayal is at hand, mental and physical torment follow. The disciples are nonplussed. Then we come across the mysterious disciple whom Jesus loved. More often than not it is applied to John himself, the author of the gospel, but there is also an element of him/her being each one of us as we draw close on each occasion around the communion table and receive a morsel. We are all capable of leaving the table, leaving Jesus and letting Him down. It is in our human nature and we do. Even within the covenant of marriage we can let our partner down. Judas, far from being spirit filled is possessed by something else, some darker side of his nature and it was dark, too, when he went out. In His own way and in His own time Jesus, the light, would overcome that darkness and Judas would not be able to stand against it. He

1. Stephen Verney, *Into the New Age* (Zondervan, 1976).

hanged himself, we are told in Matt 27:3, or blew up in Acts 1:18. At least Matthew accords him the dignity of repentance.

Chapter 13:13 repeats chapter 12:28 and expands the theme of being glorified. The Greek word for glory (doxa—hence, doxology) has a progression of meanings and its widespread use in two sentences is almost pun-like, expanding those meanings through opinion, expectation, judgment, conclusion, vision, reputation, good report, credit, and honor to glory and splendor. Opinion: Jesus clashed with authorities over opinions on the Messiah and His destiny; so too on expectations of the Messiah. Even Judas, perhaps, tried to force Jesus' hand to rebellion by shopping Him. Judgment exists in accepting Jesus. Conclusion of this earthly ministry on the cross. Vision of Jesus risen on Easter Day. His reputation and good report is in our gospels. Credit to God's Son, honor to the church. Glory and splendor to God; Father, Son and Holy Spirit. Small wonder that the icons of the Greek Orthodox Church seek to present such glorious images of Christ. The gospel itself is full of references to people's opinion and expectations, their reports of Jesus and finally His glory, the splendor, of the groom awaiting His bride.

VERSES 33–34

Jesus continues. His disciples cannot follow Him everywhere. There are certain tasks He has to do alone, entrusted to Him by God. What they can do is follow His example of love: love one another and fulfill the law. To love one another is to love God too. This is the true heart of Christianity. "Mandatum Novum," later for "a new commandment" (15:12,17) has been corrupted to "Maundy."

As usual, impetuous Peter jumps in with both feet and is seriously rebuffed. He will be the first to deny Jesus. He has a long way to go before sentiment matches deed, but it will come as the Spirit comes. He seems a new man at Pentecost. Jesus loves us right through to the uttermost, even to the cross and life beyond.

So the individual address ends and we come to the main part of the after-dinner speech, which Judas misses.

Chapter 14

THERE IS ROOM FOR us all in the heavenly palace and the groom explains where his beloved will dwell with him. The old Eaton Hall outside Chester was so vast it was used as the officer training center during the war, and in the heyday of house parties there some guests never got from the wings to the main center all weekend! Here is something bigger, more spacious, more accommodating and more welcoming. It often strikes me, when these words are used at a funeral, how diverse people are. Yet whatever our interests, skills, achievements or failures, here is the assurance that there is ample room for us if we want to be with Jesus Christ. If anyone arrives within the first thousand years following Winston Churchill's death, they can join him in the painting room. Find an easel, but don't be frightened of a blank sheet of paper! Jesus would not lie to us and lead us astray. He has gone on ahead and all is ready and prepared. We, the bride, will make our entries in our own time to this great hall. Many mansions within the house await. House and home go together and communion is about Jesus making His home in us.

VERSE 3

There is more yet. The groom, having gone on ahead to prepare everything, will return to take the bride to himself, so both can be together. Eden now has a house that Genesis did not know about! To those who doubt like Thomas, what could be more reassuring than to know the way, the truth and the life? Only the Son can reveal the Father, but to know and see the former is to know and see the latter.

VERSE 8

Phillip still cannot picture this and the imagery begins to change a little. Father and Son are imbued with the same spirit. The energy, power and the authority of the former are not just vested in the latter, but are an integral part of Him. Work you would expect of the Father is done by the Son. These are His credentials, so believe the evidence for the sake of the work you see before you. You could say believe your experience of the Son.

VERSE 15

Belief in the groom will enable the believer to do similar and more besides.

The gift of the groom is the gift of the Holy Spirit, the Comforter or Counselor. We are called as witnesses, for that is the implication of the Greek word, but to take the word to its full meaning it also implies encouraging and helping. The agency falls on us to keep the work going, rather in the same way that responsibility falls on the best man at a wedding to stand proxy for everything but the consummation. In the absence of the groom we must speak up for him, but also act for him. Christians give their own witness when they tell their own stories of Christ in their lives. In acting for Him, the Spirit moves us, because in order to be of comfort to anyone we must draw alongside that person first, whether a bereaved neighbor, a starving child, those in hospital or prison, the AIDS victim or the stranger. You cannot see the Spirit. You cannot catch Him in a glass jar any more than you can catch the wind in a jar to pass around. Only will you know the Spirit when you acknowledge Him within you. Often we may be so close, but so far away, for aspects of the Spirit work in artists, inventors and many others besides, but go unrecognized. We are those houses. The Spirit is about movement: to bring comfort to others we have to move alongside. The Spirit also disturbs us to rouse and encourage others. As my mentor, Dewi Morgan of St Brides, Fleet Street said in a telegram (there being no emails then!) on my ordination, "May the disturbance of the Holy Spirit be with you." I hope my thoughts disturb others to think for themselves! Consider, too, the gift of the Holy Spirit as from Groom to Bride, Jesus to the Church (us), and that within marriage many actions and decisions are taken in relation to the spouse automatically being of the same mind as two become one.

VERSE 18

Partially hidden from the world, those who know Him will see Him and have life in Him. Being together in the Father is a new relationship for mankind. This is the bottom line of eternal life, but how good it is that a marriage/covenant relationship of love will go on for ever. The groom will manifest himself to his lover, to his church. The in-dwelling of the Godhead in the person negates a home for the home is in the person. To keep Jesus' word is to love Him and to be at home to Him and the Father. It is back to the beginning when God first spoke and that Word lives on in us. Chaos and darkness are banished.

VERSE 25

The last dimension to be completed is the arrival of (or advent of) the Holy Spirit in us. It is in the Spirit that we remember, just as we break bread and share the cup in memory of Him. After a break, which must only be the death of the human body, all will fall into place. The ruler of the world is the tempter, the point at which we give into ourselves, though literally at a stretch it would be the Romans, the temporal rulers of most of the known world, as it is the Romans that crucify Him. Whatever it is is of no importance. Jesus gives in to neither but is true to the Father. His obedience proves His love to the Father and indeed to the world. Such is His depth of love for His bride. God puts temptation there through Satan the Accuser in the beginning to encourage us to make choices and choose Him freely. God is in control, not at continual war with a rival in heaven. Satan is mythology, a story telling illustration that we allow to exceed ancient purposes of description. Evil is only personified in the selfish side of ourselves. Satan as tempter represents having or instigating something to accuse the soul of come the Day of Judgment in Hebrew mythology (Job 1 and 2). Over the years he has taken more root than he should!

It is in breaking the body to feed us in the bread that the groom rises above the sexual to consummate his bride—us, his church. He cannot sleep with each and every one of us, but we can take Him on board in a new, intimate, personal way. We do, indeed, slowly become one flesh with Him, so the Word continues to become flesh to dwell amongst us.

Just as there is an empathy between bride and groom, a deep trust based on love and longing, that is expressed in confidence and serenity—in a word, peace—so the peace He gives us is not of this world, but of the world of lovers. In going to the Father He is not leaving His bride, but crossing a barrier for all time to be there and here always. His contact with His bride will be forever.

Chapter 15

VERSE 1

Having studied John's gospel in some depth to feel its imagery for a series of sculptures (they were eight panels, seven feet high, on The Call of the Disciples from the narrative of the early chapters of John, and another series of eight panels on the Stations of the Cross, eight feet high from the narrative of the last chapters of John) it would seem that some of the ideas in the stories Jesus tells relate directly to the occupations of some of the disciples. He talked and taught in their idiom. Vine-dressing would have been a known art to many of them, and some, if we think of the gardener image, may have been gardeners. The picture of the way growth is encouraged is so true. In our own lives we can become conscious of the extra pruning to promote more growth still. How often are we challenged and changed yet again? Our strength is in the Lord.

The cleansing effect of the Word reminds us of the process starting with baptism. Water cleanses and nourishes. When grafting or pruning, dirt causes decay, disease and deterioration. We are one with Him, but the beauty of it is that he allows the bride to be the blossom, the follower, and the fruit, all the aspects for which the vine is admired. Again the imagery of water reminds us of the destructive power of water, the Red Sea experience where those pleasing to God passed through but those displeasing to God were overwhelmed. There are two options: life in the groom, or cut off, rejected and thrown on the bonfire. The blossom demands food of the vine via the leaves and the roots. The bride, if fed and nurtured by the groom and the vinedresser, is honored by a good crop. The complete circle of love between all parties will ensure the joy of all concerned.

(Paul uses the gardener's image of grafting rather differently in Rom 12:17.)

VERSE 12

Matt 19:19; 5:43; 22:37; Mark 12:29; and Luke 10:27:

If we recall the "Shema," the call to worship, that Jesus quoted ("Love God with all you've got and your neighbor as yourself") then Jesus' new commandment is just as compelling. As God loves us in and through Jesus Christ, then we must reciprocate to fulfill the first command and the second. In loving others we fulfill the first commandment too. If we think of Matt 25:3 to end on judgment then we have an example of loving one another and loving Jesus too. Would that the prisoner could discern the hand of Christ though those who love Him, could learn forgiveness, and not set out to get those who shopped Him on being released. (Such was the first objective of one man I visited in prison when he was released.)

VERSE 13

How often is this verse quoted on Remembrance Sunday—or Armistice Day as it may become if it adheres to 11.00 a.m. on the eleventh day of the eleventh month: "Greater love has no man than this, that a man lay down his life for his friends." Read any of the memories of any of the fighter pilots—Hill, Johnston, Lucas, Dundas and others—and reflect on their policy of drinking the health of absent friends on their return from a mission, as mentioned earlier. Is not this almost Eucharistic giving thanks for them and remembering their sacrifice? In my years as a serving officer and as a regimental padre, I found this attitude particularly poignant when dealing with Remembrance Sunday. Drinking their health allies them to the groom who bids us drink his health in memory of him. So even if it was not my war, it was for me too. The Tomb of the Unknown Soldier is a poignant reminder.

VERSE 14–17

We are elevated to friends, indeed finally brothers, not servants, slaves and cannon fodder. The Word from God has been passed on to us and given to us. We are chosen, we are appointed, we are fertilized to produce lasting fruit. In itself that is one interpretation of the strand of eternal life that binds us all together. It is garden imagery again.

VERSES 18 TO THE END

Thus united to Christ, we run the risk of sharing the same reactions of others to Him. Hated for Him if we love Him, the more so because He chose us. Being in the world but not of the world sets us apart "holy, a royal priesthood," to quote 1 Pet 2:5. As the master is treated, so is the servant. Sin (falling short, missing the mark as in archery) exists because the truth is now evident in Christ. As Paul argues, the law exposed sin, so too, Christ exposes those who reject Him. They make a choice, not a gamble, but they lose life. And to hate Christ is not just to hate those who share his mantle but to hate God the Father too. Psalms 35:19 and 69:4 are not without their irony and like all scripture it is fulfilled in Christ. Life or rejection: another aspect of eternal life as opposed to outer darkness or nothingness. Almost Unitarian in his summing up, the Holy Spirit is included. When Jesus says "sent by him from the Father" in verse 26, it suggests the Greek Orthodox original of the Nicene Creed, "Who proceeds from the Father through the Son," but when He goes on to say this "Spirit of truth, who proceeds from the Father," we find that we are quoting the Romanized version we have adopted of the creed, the very words He said. What big muddles are made of small things? Surely there is room for both, side by side as both appear to exist here!

So we are called to be witnesses. The groom exhorts his audience and warns his bride that like many wives, whatever ridicule or rejection or pressure the husband undergoes or receives, the wife will feel it too. To be witnesses we are called to baptism, as at the start of the gospel. We recognize the groom, for the spirit of truth bears witness and we are commissioned to proclaim the truth. The Counselor will fire us up.

Although John does not specifically mention the Lord's Prayer as part of Jesus' teaching opens, the spirit of "Thy Kingdom come, they will be done" is very much contained in his after-dinner speech—a very appropriate time for the groom to speak. Here I find the sense of the pictorial image given at the start of the gospel, with Jesus' baptism and John the Baptist at work pointing out Jesus to his disciples (John 1:40). If we understand that John's baptism in the River Jordan caused people to re-enter the promised land, then here we have Jesus' teaching taking us a stage further to enter the Kingdom of God. This Kingdom is bounded by no more than the river of baptism and exists wherever God rules our hearts.

Chapter 16

VERSE 1–4

It may be a salutary lesson, or even persecution, that prompts us to remember the groom's words. How many people how often reject the groom we know? What about those sects that reject or abuse Christ's teaching in God's name? If we distort God then we will find His behavior, or rather action in His name distorted. God has spoken to us and the Word has taken our flesh. We are all called!

VERSES 5–11

Now the sayings get harder to unravel and appear to undermine what is just becoming an established relationship. How can a contract appear to continue if one of the parties immediately talks about going away? One of the blessings is that despite absence the contract holds good and strengthens the parties to it. To fetch and to give his gift, the groom has to go and get it! The counselor, the comforter, the helper will be with us all always. Through this spirit we shall evaluate life. He will convince the world. The word also means "reprove." He will correct the world. Sin, righteousness and judgment have to be put into perspective and held in the right balance (one of the judges' complaints against the Home Secretary about fixed sentences—the punishment needs to fit the crime). Sin is clearly in existence when people fail to believe in the groom. Righteousness is about going in the right direction; towards the

Father led by Christ. If the groom leads the bride to consummate the marriage, she has to trust him, follow him and consent to him. Judgment is present in what rules the world. Our selfishness and desire to please ourselves is sublimated to "I do": consent to someone beyond and outside ourselves but part of us. It is not so much Frankie Howerd,[1] "and so to bed," but the two become one flesh. Communion does it for us.

VERSES 12–15

Here is the witness that John is leading us to and the groom describing: the Spirit of Truth. Our eyes are being opened. After Christ the Spirit takes the Word God utters and passes it on. In a way, the witness that was John (and there is much about baptism in the early chapters that absorbs him into the gospel to build on his pointer) is now the Holy Spirit in us.

VERSES 16–24

What Jesus nips away to do with the Father is to open up direct dialogue with Him. Ask in His name and the Father will give it. What greater gift could the groom bestow on his bride and guests to fulfill their joy?

VERSES 25–30

From where He comes, thence He must return. The earlier stuff of eternal life, "to have seen and loved me is to love the Father," is reciprocated in that to love Christ is to be loved by the Father. Thus, the penny finally drops for the disciples!

1. The comedian's quote was from his commentary in the comedy 'Up Pompeii'.

VERSES 31–END

Yet Jesus warns the disciples there is more in store for them yet. They may believe now but they will find it harder. He will be alone; they will be scattered. Yet just as He has the Father with Him for consolation and strength, so they will find peace and consolation through Him and in Him. The world remains the world, but Jesus is above the world. Disaster and affliction will no longer bind us. God may refine us and we may bring adversity upon ourselves, but Jesus' prayer that follows reflects, "lead us not into temptation, but deliver us from evil." "Do not bring me to the time of trial but deliver us from the evil one," which is a literal translation of Matthew.

Chapter 17

JESUS CONCLUDES HIS SPEECH with prayer; prayer to be glorified (vv.1–5); prayer for the disciples (vv.6–19); and prayer for the church (vv.20–26).

VERSES 1–5

Not so much back to basics, as back to the beginning. As in Proverbs 8, the Word or wisdom was at the creator's side at the very beginning. Creation as we know it is God's glory. Jesus' achievement as our Lord and Christ is His glory and this reflects on the Father. The gift and the glory are eternal life. Eternal life is to know God and Son. The process is continuous, rather as the Seventh Day, God's rest (see Ps 95) as the Sabbath day of rest is continuous. The glory stretches to heaven again from earth and completes this fullness of God's grace. The groom's work will then be complete, just as Drake's prayers suggest:

> "Disturb us, Lord, to dare more boldly, To venture on wider seas where storms will show your mastery; Where losing sight of land, We shall find the stars. We ask You to push back the horizons of our hopes; and to push into the future In strength, courage, hope and love."

And:

> "O Lord God, when thou givest to thy servants to endeavor any great matter, grant us also to know it is not

> the beginning but the continuing of the same unto the end until it be thoroughly finished, which yields the true glory; through Him who for the finishing of thy work laid down His life, our Redeemer Jesus Christ."

VERSES 6–19

Manifesting is revealing or making known (also an epiphany), but we would understand it better in terms of "living out." Jesus' prayer is specially for those who believe Him. To know the name is to know the person. Jesus has revealed God's name and nature as Father, so let Him keep those for whom He prays. It is a prayer worthy for all ordinations. The joy of the groom needs to be reflected by the rest present. With God at work through those to whom Jesus has given His word, evil cannot run riot without check. "Deliver us from the evil me" is part of this prayer. Our sanctification in the truth is through the Word of God in Jesus. We are consecrated in Christ by His success.

VERSES 20–END

Jesus goes on to pray for those to whom the Word reaches through those He has set up. This is the nature and the structure and the being of his bride us. One flesh with the groom through this mystic consummation makes us one flesh with the Father. All are one in the Spirit, the subject of many a modern chorus. The Spirit is also the glory, so thus attired or arrayed or clothed is the appropriate idiom for us to consider ourselves so endowed. While the groom cannot physically spread himself throughout His church, He can do so in spirit and through communion. We can glimpse something of the heavenly feast, something of a return to Eden through baptism and entering the Kingdom of God, and something of the heavenly splendor, as we consider Jesus' redeeming work completed and the Trinity triumphant. As we take Christ on board in communion, so He is in us and God's love is in us. Thus are we made more in the image of God. In fact it is through the Church, us, that God is seen.

So having prayed and filled the glass with himself, and having drunk from it, the groom prepares to smash the glass—to die on the cross—which I have used as a symbol through this commentary. These prayers sum up the groom's willingness to enter into the marriage covenant with his Church. It is the equivalent of the Ketubah.

Chapter 18

So Judas finds Jesus after supper in one of His favorite haunts and leads others to arrest Him. Even so they are in awe of Him. Twice nothing happens and a third time Peter lashes out. Sadly we hear no more of Malchus after this traumatic experience. Jesus loses none of His companions in a fight: verse 9 echoes His prayer for His disciples (17:12). However, there is no further mention of Judas by John. Before the sacrifice Jesus is drinking very deeply indeed of the cup (v.11): "Shall I not drink of the cup which the Father has given me?" Also see 19:28—a hint of the imagery of the cup, "I thirst." The agony in Gethsemane is more fully recounted in the synoptic gospels, but in the end, "Thy will be done." The Old Testament is full of imagery of God's wrath contained in a cup of foaming wine. (Cup of Wrath: Isa 51:17. Cup of Salvation: Ps 116:13; Jer 25:15; Hab 2:15. Cup of Blessing: 1 Cor 10:16; Rev 16:19; Pss 16:5, 23:5 and 75:8.) The Cup of Judgment becomes the Cup of Salvation for us at Holy Communion. Only Ps 23:5 hints at the champagne reception and celebration when all is complete: "My cup overflows. . ."

Firstly, Jesus is taken to Annas, who as father-in-law of the high priest seems to hold the power.

VERSE 14

John is very specific about Caiaphas' prophecy that it is expedient for one man to die for the people. Here Old Testament and New

Testament merge as the prophecies concerning Jesus continue to be made and fulfilled. (See John 11:44–50.)

VERSES 15–27

Peter denies Christ, obviously very much in the presence of another disciple (vv.15–16). Who this disciple is, is not clear. Popularly he is identified with John and the disciple whom Jesus loved. It indicates with some certainty the cross-section from which Jesus drew His disciples, His groomsmen.

As everything appears to fall apart, will the groom's love win the day and hold everything together? Not only has Judas betrayed Him but His "number one" is ducking his head below the parapet and is distancing himself. Half drawn towards his master, he equally as much is keen to disassociate himself too.

Jesus' defense when questioned implies there are those amongst His accusers who could answer the questions they ask themselves. They are privy to all the talk we have had recounted by John and the deeds surrounding the words. They cannot back up their arguments nor refute His theology. Jesus has hidden nothing. "There's none so blind as them that cannot see," is the old adage.

VERSE 27

Jesus' prophecy concerning Peter's denial is fulfilled (John 13:37–38).

VERSES 28–38

We don't know what took place at Caiaphas' house, but by the time Jesus was before Pilate at the praetorium they had already decided to put Him to death. However, politically they needed the Romans to pass the death penalty. Jesus presents a summary of much of His after dinner speech as an explanation to Pilate. He was born in the world to bear witness to the truth. There is a hint of Jesus' reply to the disciples and those who arrested Him in Matthew's version that if it was not to be, the armies of angels would have rescued Him (Matt 26:51–56). Pilate has missed Jesus' teaching: "What is truth?" The irony is the truth has still to come out and it is one of his centurions (Mark 15:39) who notices it.

VERSES 39–40

Is it coincidence or a final irony that the robber has a similar name, Barabbas, son of the father? It is certainly convenient for stirring up and misleading a crowd in case there is doubt about who should be released. However, it works out that the Son of Man is relegated to the lowest ranks, which is one interpretation of the title: lowest man.

Chapter 19

In the context, the breaking of the glass is no pleasant experience. Indeed, Jesus is ground down by the Roman and the Jewish heel. The scenario is rich with confrontation between the Roman and Jewish authorities. Just when Pilate thinks he has done enough to punish Jesus and satisfy the Jews with the mocking irony of "Behold the Man," the Jews call his bluff. As Son of Man, or more particularly as the Word made flesh now grown from babyhood to manhood, it is a raw presentation of God in earthly form. Not venerated nor adored, but He is mocked.

VERSE 8

As Son of God, the chief priests reckon He ought to die. Here we have the Son of God with Pilate almost pleading with Him. Where are you from? Was He greater than Caesar after all?

VERSES 10–11

Pilate almost has the earthly power of God when it comes to absolute rule. Jesus lets him off the hook. The power is from above and that is clearly God. The person who delivered Him to Pilate is more difficult to identify. Some would say it is Caiaphas who is now doomed, other sources would go for Judas who is on course for perdition, but I would favor those human instruments whom

God who has used to work through the situation to fulfill His purpose. God is not a sinner but He does have control over sin if He can put the world under Satan. Furthermore, it is said with the same breath as the allusion to who has the power from above. Therefore, suggesting God at the first, it is presumably God in the second instance in order to take on and remove the sin. So Jesus' pain is identified with God's pain for the world. Pilate would see authority from above as Caesar in the first instance. The Jews, by special dispensation of the Romans, enjoyed religious toleration so if their faith demanded death, that would be the way the cookie had to crumble. Pilate has to go with the flow, however uncomfortable. God is still in control.

VERSES 17–22

The dissenting continues and there is more controversy over the title Pilate put on the cross. On the one hand it is Roman contempt for the Jews, anti-Semitism, and on the other the Jews are trying to fix the blame squarely on Jesus so they could claim His own words betrayed Him. Just as the title was written and remained unchanged, so what John wrote about Jesus has been passed down unchanged for two thousand years, the very record of what Jesus said and did. It is a good contrast to the thieves (Luke 23:39–43), who argue about Jesus in their lives at this point.

VERSES 23–27

The seamless garment is kept whole and scripture fulfilled as the soldiers cast lots for it (Ps 22:18). I would like someone to research more the nature and significance of His raiment. We get too much of children in pajamas and tea-towels on their heads etc. at nativity plays to know the full impact of His tunic. It would appear to be a sort of poncho or similar over garment.

Jesus commends His mother to John's safekeeping: it is worth a visit to their last house at Ephesus (by which time Mary must have been extremely old!). Even if only folklore, it is a meeting point of Christian and Muslim faiths because for the latter it is a shrine to the prophet's mother. Indeed, Muslim women go there to pray for safe childbearing. That fact alone authenticates it enough! Of the women with Mary, some would say his mother's sister was Salome the mother of James and John and wife of Zebedee, and the second Mary, wife of Clopas, the mother of James the younger and Joses. Were Clopas and Mary the two on the road to Emmaus in Luke's gospel 24:13–35? Of Mary Magdalene, more anon, but she was not a lady of ill repute as some would say and confuse her with the woman who washed Jesus' feet with her tears, Luke 7:36–50, and compare that with John 12:1–8 and the same anointing by Mary of Bethany in the synoptics.

VERSES 28–33

Psalms fill out the theme. The groom has drunk the bitter potion and the glass is crushed. In His thirst on the cross He has laid the seeds of the thirst of the world that has been drinking of Him ever since. For those who want to follow further the theme of this cup that Jesus must drink as a taster and cupbearer, see Pss 11:6, 16:5, 75:8 and 116:13, where it is called the cup of salvation. (Ps 23:5 points to the Messiah, the anointed one.) Isa 51 is particularly rich in the metaphor of the cup, so that the actions of the groom fill out these words. Jer 25 picks up this theme; also 49:12. Ezekiel 23 puts this theme in a very forthright manner, comparing the unfaithfulness of Samaria and Jerusalem. He who has drunk this cup removes all desolation, and in a way we can see holy communion as a continuation of drinking the cup to keep any judgment at bay. Hab 2:15–16 also weaves in this imagery of the cup of wrath. Paul (1 Cor 10 and 11) puts the cup in the context of communion and partaking worthily, and John in Rev 14:10, 16:19, 17:4 and 18:6 expands the theme. The cup of seduction: too much drink and the occasion can deteriorate to debauchery not celebration. We live and practice our faith on a knife edge. Not for nothing was adultery used in the Old Testament to describe departure from God. The cup of judgment has become the cup of Salvation.

So Jesus, having drunk, utters, "It is finished."

Again, in the words of Ps 22:17–18 (in fact, read the whole psalm in the light of the crucifixion for it is packed with description of the event: verses 6–8, the torment; verses 9–10, His mother is there) puts the action in the context of the prophecies that are fulfilled and Jesus is left in one piece on the cross, being dead. Verse 34: then one of the soldiers pierces His side with a spear and out comes blood and water. I am no medic, but if a lung is pierced then fluid might well come out if it has accumulated and the crucified person has in the sense drowned or suffocated, because crucifixion made breathing difficult and the person was reduced to writhing. It also combines Ps 34:20 and Zech 12:10, themes of rejection and restoration, but also the source of living water opened up like by Moses' staff in Sinai (Exod 17:1–7). In fact the rock round Horeb is porous and mineral salts form a crust where moisture has evaporated, so by striking the rock Moses removes the crust and water can flow.

VERSES 34–37

But John is trying to tell us more. With the broken flesh there is water and blood; the water and wine of communion, the stream of living water, and within the context of this meditation the water made wine in the broken vessel, the glass broken by the groom after he has drained it (compare two cups and holy communion in Luke's gospel at the Last Supper). For John it is another pointer to the truth that Jesus is the Son of God. However we reflect on it, whatever adds to the picture John paints and convinces us further is a help. The Word made flesh may have been silent as a baby in a manger (Matthew and Luke) but we remember Him for His parables, His teaching and words from the cross. Mindful of Eve made from Adam's rib (Gen 2) it is possible to read in a link with Jesus' side being pierced and opened up to release His body for His bride, the church. It is also worth considering the poetry of the Bible that we can enter into a marriage; as God divided Adam to make Eve, so we complete His creativity by becoming one flesh once more as husband and wife.

VERSES 38–END

So come Joseph of Arimathea and Nicodemus, who appeared in the third chapter and now makes another appearance in the third last chapter, and they take the body away for burial with a vast weight of spices for embalming. John stressed the crucifixion took place on the day of preparation, the day when the lamb for the Passover feast is slaughtered. It is also worth considering the logistics and proximity of city wall, cross and tomb. Were you to be in or under the Church of the Holy Sepulchre in Jerusalem, this would make more sense. Not only can one consider the distance the cross might be carried from the citadel to Golgotha, but also the proximity of Caiaphas' house to the citadel of David where Herod and Pilate both had rooms or its use. The Romans and the Jews would want to consider the shortest and safest routes in case a rescue attempt should be mounted. At the end of the day, before the Sabbath and holy day began, the distance from cross to tomb must be very short. Thus while General Gordon's choice of garden tomb evokes the right sort of feel, the distance is too great. The smoky chapels within the great Holy Sepulchre church hold the clues, with high ground outside the city wall on the right as you enter (thus from the wall people could spit at Jesus on the cross) for Golgotha, and the tomb in the undercrypt there that covers the old quarry, new tombs and a picture advertising a fish shop with the sign of the fishing boat.

Chapter 20

Resurrection

According to the criteria of Paul, who states that seeing the risen Christ and being sent as a witness by Him is the qualification to be an apostle, Mary Magdalene must be the first apostle. To see and be sent. Paul's road to Damascus experience is the classic type, but all the disciples saw and were sent personally, as was Mary in the garden. Certainly her following Jesus and devotion to Him awards the status of honorary disciple to begin with, and female at that! (Eph 3:3—revelation; of divine origin, seal of apostleship. See Acts 22: 6–18, 26:13–18 and 9:1–31; Gal 1:11–24; 1 Cor 9:1). Mistaking Jesus as the gardener I find gives an ironic twist to Jesus words in chapter 15:1—"my father is the vinedresser." We can also puzzle over the disciple whom Jesus loved seeing the linen cloths, entering the tomb after Peter and eventually believing. The scene is an empty tomb, save for the linen cloths and the napkin which had been on Jesus' head. As a priest, I rather equate these with used purificators after administering communion, when the chalice is empty and cleaned and the linen is folded away. It suggests a body has not been stolen or struggled, but the exit (Exodus) is ordered.

VERSES 1–18

Jesus' words to Mary apply to us all. "Do not hold me. . ." and "go and tell the others. . ." We are very inclined to pull Jesus down to us and clasp Him, but we must let Him ascend and look up to Him. Rather than bring Him down, we must reach up. Secondly, we must go and tell others the truth—our Father, our God. Our Lord. Now is the groom's message to us, his bride, taking shape, and Mary is the first recipient of it and the first to do the risen Lord's bidding. Again as a priest, having administered communion, those recipients of it need to go forth and do their bit too. We could identify Mary Magdalene as a symbol of the Church, the Bride. In sculpture I would see Mary the Mother as the mythical Mother Earth figure and Mary Magdalene as the mythical fertility figure: one has born the Word, the other has carried it out.

VERSES 19–24

Jesus then appears to the ten disciples, for Thomas is absent, and pours out His Spirit on them, literally, "Receive Holy Spirit." It is their baptism according to John's gospel. It is as if they have drunk deeply from His cup and now, instead of reeling and staggering (or being accused of being drunk, as in Luke's Acts 2:13) they are strengthened from on high and stand full square with the groom they have been accompanying. They are baptized, they acclaim Jesus with their response, and they are commissioned to go out and proclaim Him. They are full-blown witnesses, apostles in every sense.

VERSES 24–END

Eight days later, doubting Thomas, called the Twin, is with them when Jesus calls, having first denied his colleagues' story. If those who were with Jesus disbelieve their story, then they will have a jolly time of it when they go out to reclaim Him! However the second "coming" of Jesus (is there a message here from John?) to them convinces Thomas and acts like a bridge to subsequent generations who are not lucky enough to have seen Jesus (v.29: "Blessed are those who have not seen and yet believe.") Notice that in verse 8 the disciple whom Jesus loved and outran Peter waited outside for him and after him entered and saw and believed.

We still remember His cup and His words and perpetuate His memory. Through what He has given us He remains as alive to us as to them then.

VERSES 30–31

As a postscript, John mentions the purpose of his gospel is to ensure we and others have life in Christ through belief in Him as Son of God. The words of the groom have been presented as the Word of God to convince us. In a society with any culture, its fertility and reproduction must be preceded by an acceptance, by "I do" and consent. Where we believe the Word, when uttered, darkness and chaos are dispelled, so that same Word, the church's and our groom, dispels darkness in life today by soliciting our favorable response.[1]

1. The Lamb of God pointed out to Andrew 1.v29 coincides with the word of the angels to the shepherds in Luke 2,v12 where: 'they will find a babe wrapped in swaddling clothes lying in a manger.' If shepherds had a new-born lamb without blemish they wrapped it in swaddling clothes and laid it in a manger to keep it clean and pure for sacrifice, no doubt for a good price. Also reflect that Lazarus had to be unbound from his funeral wraps whereas Jesus' shroud was neatly folded.

Chapter 21
The Epilogue

VERSES 1–14

JESUS APPEARS TO THE disciples who have gone fishing. I feel this draft of fishes complements the occasion of Peter's call in the synoptic gospels (Matt 18:14–22; Mark 1:16–20; Luke 5:1–11). I don't begin to understand 153 in number. The best explanation is that it is an acrostic, rather like "ICHTHUS." It is also a prime number and a combination number for those into numbers! Then again, on a vulgar level the fish was a phallic symbol for the ancient Greeks, so could there be an ironic joke that it is also the symbol for a new fertility of the Spirit-filled? Another mystery is that Jesus when He breaks bread and feeds people also seems to offer fish (v.13), as in feeding the five thousand (6:11). Fish seems to have no part of modern day ritual or worship but was the meat or flesh of those days. On another level the disciples are going to have to cast their nets wide. (Nathanael is of Cana (v.2), so perhaps it was his wedding in chapter 2?)

VERSES 15–19

Jesus questions Peter, who in turn quizzes Jesus about the disciple whom Jesus loved following. Feeding lambs, tending sheep and feeding sheep have a particular rural ring about them for they are all separated tasks, yet linked. Some would say it is to purge Peter of his threefold denial, but more obviously if you feed lambs then they grow into sheep and need further nurture and feed. The nature of pastoral work is ongoing and continuous, not a one-off at a time. It is a lesson for the future about God's love and His love at work through us. Wherever it may lead (v.18), such shepherding in the good shepherd's name can only happen if we follow Him (v.19). As an aside: why did God favor Abel's gift over Cain's? Shepherding and care of stock is a full time job, and also deals with life-blood. Cain was a tiller of the soil so having sown could sit back while God's creativity got it growing.

We are all naked before God and Peter's threefold denial of Christ strips him naked, so to speak. Here the risen Christ appears to re-cloth Peter and re-install him. He ceases to be so impetuous and more solid. For more on Peter, read Mark's gospel and how he takes the lead in Acts.

VERSES 20–23

Is there doubt about this special disciple? Or is there a temptation to elevate him after Jesus? Whatever Peter's thoughts on the matter and on how this beloved disciple is reacting to Jesus, the command from Jesus to Peter is straightforward: "Follow me" (v.22). Equally puzzling is "Remaining until I come" (vv.22–23). Although close to Jesus, perhaps this man is not convinced at the time in the sense that Jesus has not come to him; He has not taken him on board yet so Peter is quizzical. By the time the gospel is written there is no further convincing necessary. He had to remain for a task and that task, entrusted to a special friend, has been for our benefit, so verses 24 and 25 speak for themselves. John found belief in the empty tomb. His gospel, that he remained to write, enables Jesus to come (again) to others. "Until I come" hints at a personal second coming when the individual accepts Jesus. It is not for those with Spirit to worry about those that remain. We cannot hasten the Spirit in others, we can only point them to Christ. God calls and the Holy Spirit may lead Christ to come again in them. One day all will be complete in God.

St John's Gospel Synopsis for Meditation

Central theme pivots on Wedding at Cana because this becomes allegorical of the relation of Christ and us the church: groom and bride. Of Jewish wedding: Christ, vehicle of the wine sealing the union, i.e. broken like the glass.

The prominent "I AM" sayings give us the character of the Groom.

A timeline of the main points.

Chapter 1

We are introduced to the groom: the Word: the Light. These themes recur. Baptism was in the wilderness, but no forty days.

Also we have the *evidence* of the best man: John the Baptist. This bears fruit as Andrew and Philip find Jesus and bring another along, Peter and Nathanael.

Chapter 2—Wedding: Nathanael of Cana?

The wine is a recurring symbol. . .

Temple cleansed: raise it in three days. It becomes an accusation against Jesus.

FIRST SIGN:

Chapter 3—Fruit of the Union

Spiritual birth, baptism water and spirit: Nicodemus.
Further testament by John.

Chapter 4—More Fruit: Samaria

Jesus accused of being Samarian. Official's son healed at Capernaum. ("I am" living water.)

SECOND SIGN:

Chapter 5—Lame Man healed at Bethesda on Sabbath

When the water is troubled the first in is restored, but here water of life takes over to stretch the imagery.

THIRD SIGN:

Deeds and scripture point to Jesus and witness to Him, as does the Father (vv.30–47).

He is resurrection of life. He describes His mission from the Father to give life.

Jesus describes himself as Son of Man and is the resurrection of judgment whereby those who believe in Him are saved (5:25–29).

Chapter 6—Feed the Five Thousand

(All gospels)

Lux Mundi: "I am the light of the World" (8:12).
Jesus the breadwinner.
Jesus walks on sea: experience of baptism (Ps 107).
Jesus as "bread of life," "I am" (6:35).

FOURTH AND FIFTH SIGNS (NOT LUKE):

Chapter 7—Jesus as "Water of Life" ("I am")

See Ezekiel fulfilled as living water flows.

Chapter 8—Woman Caught in Adultery

Biggest threat to marriage.

Yet also combines Jesus' attitude to judgment and forgiveness.
Jesus LIGHT OF THE WORLD.
Chosen people—children of Abraham

Chapter 9—Healing the Blind Man

Farce in the temple!

SIXTH SIGN:

Again, Jesus describes himself "Son of Man." "I am" (10:9) gate of sheepfold.

Chapter 10—Jesus as the Good Shepherd

"I am" (10:11) Good Shepherd.

(Old Testament imagery: Zechariah).
Jesus as "Son of God": more opposition from the Jews.

Chapter 11—Raising of Lazarus: Jesus the Resurrection and the Life

"I am" the resurrection and the life (11:25).

SEVENTH SIGN:

Caiaphas' prophecy.

Chapter 12—Jesus Anointed

Palm Sunday (all four Gospels).
Verses 44–50: to reject Jesus' word is to be judged.

Chapter 13: Example: Foot washing: service

Reaction of the disciples.

Chapters 14–16: Last Supper Discourse

Many mansions: much room: much variety:
I AM THE WAY, THE TRUTH AND THE LIFE (14:6).
The Holy Spirit promised.
"I am the true vine" (15:1).

Chapter 17—Christ's High Priestly Prayer

All four Gospels.

Chapter 18—Betrayal and Arrest

"I am" the way, the truth and the life.
All four Gospels.

Chapter 19—Jesus Condemned, Crucified, Dead and Buried

THE GLASS IS BROKEN.

ALL FOUR GOSPELS:

Chapter 20—Jesus' Resurrection

Chapter 21—Jesus reappears to disciples fishing

Threefold charge to Peter:

- Feed my lambs.
- Tend my sheep.
- Feed my sheep.

Disciples whom Jesus loved (from Chapter 13).
Remaining until Jesus comes: advent to individual.
Some of the parts make up the whole!
(Church/bride: Ezek 16.)

The Final Word

PSALM 75: THE CUP OF WRATH AND JUDGMENT

We thank You, God; Your works declare You're close.
When in charge I shall judge rightly; people shift,
They're weak so I hold them up. I tell fools
To keep Your covenant, observe the rules;
Beware of pride, shun haughtiness. No lift
In life is to be found for the morose.
God is judge as He says and He decides
Who to promote or put down. Their merits
Are weighed. He holds a cup full of red wine
From which He pours: for the elect it's fine,
The ungodly get the dregs. Their spirits
Fall short and instead it's them God derides.
Thus I say God's judgment is fair, the proud
Toppled, the faithful with salvation endowed.

PSALM 116: THE CUP OF BLESSING AND SALVATION

I'm pleased the Lord heard my prayer, therefore
I shall address Him always all my days.
I felt like death, as if drawn down to hell:
When so troubled I beseeched the Lord to quell
My anxiety for deliverance pays:
The Lord is gracious, we praise Him more.
He preserves the simple: when in misery
He helped me, He exercises mercy.
I will walk before Him 'mongst the living.
How can I reward the Lord's benefits?
I will receive the cup of salvation.
I'll speak publicly, avoid temptation;
Having freedom I'll serve Him as befits.
I'll offer Him sacrifices of thanksgiving.

From my collection on each Psalm, *Psalmody*.[1]

1. Toddy Hoare, *Psalmody* (Eugene, OR: Resource, 2024).

A NOTE ON THE TYPE

The typeface used is Minion Pro derived from late Renaiassance classic typefaces by Adobe designer Robert Slimbach in 1990 to be versatile but clear enough for digital technology, yet flexible for a range of uses.

www.ingramcontent.com/pod-product-compliance
Lightning Source LLC
LaVergne TN
LVHW020649100826
845148LV00012B/2396